Bra*in*sights

USE NEUROSCIENCE TO LIVE, LOVE, AND LEAD A BETTER LIFE

By

DAVID C WINEGAR

Original Artwork by Kati Immonen

Black and White Economy Edition

ISBN 978-952-94-1464-2

DEDICATION

I would like to dedicate this book first to my family for their support and encouragement in taking on this project.

I would also like to thank all the neuroscience researchers who I know have made significant personal sacrifices to bring us insights into our brains. They are remarkable, and I would like to extend my gratitude to them for their hard work and dedication.

Lastly, I would like to thank all my supporters on Publisizer who inspired me to make this book the best it could possibly be. My sincere thanks go out to each one of you:

Jen Bell, Marina Dieck, Jacek Franuz, Ekaterina Frolova, John Garner, Michael Green, Josef Gross, Thomas Gylling, Nora Härme, Ruedi Habermacher, Minna Hyvätti, Kati Immonen, Pekka Innanen, Pirjo Jääskeläinen, Deb Johnson, Anneli Karlstedt, Markku Leskinen, Leena Liimatainen, Patrik Lundbaeck, Jukka Mäki, Ludger Marekwia, Telmo Marques, Sabit Nasretdin, Carol Nycklemoe, Kimmo Nyman, Shyam Pathak, Richard Pyle, Heikki Rannikko, Lukas Renlund, Mark Rufer, Cindy Shi, Tracy Stevenson-Olson, Miia Taanila, Marjatta Takala, Giovanni Vaccaro, Jaakko Vilen, Alan Winegar, Bradford Winegar, Deanna Winegar, Charles Winegar.

A special thank you to Tuomas Saastamoinen and Thomas Gylling at Konecranes for their corporate sponsorship and support of my work.

Table of Contents

PREFACE

We are at a remarkable time in human history where the black box that is our brain is giving up its secrets. For the 40 000 years the modern human mind has existed (Simon Neubauer 2018), it has mostly been an enigma. We knew very little about the actual workings of the brain, and we struggled to understand the processes influencing our behavior. We are now moving out of a dark age into a period of enlightenment – a period of rapid and bountiful discovery led by technological advances and a 50 000-strong army of neuroscientists.

Neuroscience is responsible for the study of the structure and function of the nervous system and brain. Neuroscientists are exploring the workings of our minds in numerous fields, from the study of neurological disorders to consumer marketing, helping us to understand the origins and drivers of our behavior.

This new body of research has emerged only in the last 20 years. It is the direct result of advancements in brain imaging made possible through the invention of new brain imaging technologies such as the functional magnetic resonance imaging (fMRI) machine.

My goal in writing this book is to help you understand the latest neuroscience studies. I want to open your eyes to what the research is telling about your brains and help you use this knowledge to live, love, and lead your life to the fullest.

Some might consider this a 'self-help' book, but I dislike the term because books in this category are so often pitched as a 'magic bullet' to how to be better. I won't give you the 'three steps to a better life.' What I will give you is science-based insight into how your brain works and the implications for your life.

Admittedly, the science this book is based on is complicated. What makes the science difficult to understand is the overwhelming amount of terminology. To help make the science more accessible, I have chosen not to go too deep into the scientific jargon. It is not my intention to 'dumb-down' this book but to make this more accessible by explaining the concepts without the use of all the heavy words.

When we understand our brains better, we have the power to move our lives in new directions. Our minds are remarkable in their ability to create new connections, process large volumes of information, automate complicated tasks, and acquire exceptional new skills.

By embracing the research, we open ourselves to new possibilities. Possibilities which can profoundly impact how we live and interact with others, orientating our brains to work in ways better in sync with how they have evolved. We can learn to 'hack' our brains and maximize their potential for greatness.

How to use this book

If wisdom is organized life and science organized knowledge, art is

organized beauty

Immanuel Kant

I wrote this book to inform, enlighten, and inspire you to use neuroscience to improve your understanding of yourself and others. It is not a traditional self-help book. It is not a simple three-step method, but a book that will take you inside your mind and provide insight into what motivates your behavior. By understanding what triggers certain behavior, you gain the ability to control and change it and the possibility to influence others.

The brain is infused with emotion, and I aspired to make emotion more than words on paper with this book. I have worked with a professional watercolorist, the brilliant Kati Immonen, to produce the original artwork for this book.

The artwork serves as a symbol of the section it proceeds, not literal. The art does not represent parts of the brains or brain systems, but is here to stimulate your mind, to activate emotions and help you feel some of what is going on in your brain every moment of your life as you experience new things.

I would encourage you to take a few minutes before the start of each section and focus on the art. Dive deep into the image – a lot is going on – and let your brain get lost in it. Let it trigger your emotional brain and let the feelings wash over you. Use it as a point of meditation to relax before digging into the research. By calming your brain, you will find yourself open to new ideas and be able to appreciate better how to apply neuroscience concepts to your life.

When you complete each section, return to that section's image and take time processing what you have just learned. The brain needs time to filter and commit to memory. Give it time, and you will find you remember more and can use what you remember to improve your life.

SIMPLICITY = BEAUTY

*Science is beautiful when it makes simple explanations of phenomena
or connections between different observations.*

Stephen Hawking

Admittedly, I will oversimplify many subjects in this book. The human brain is complex by nature. I could write volumes on the structure of the brain alone. What is more important to understand are the implications of the research and how it can be used to understand behavior.

Neuroscience provides us with clues into how and why we do what we do. We can use this information to orchestrate our behaviors and interactions to be more productive. Information is power. Insight into the workings of the human brain is *power squared.*

The brain prefers to get from point A to point B as quickly as possible. By cutting out the jargon and complexity, I hope I get you to the destination of how you can use this research to make a change in your life.

I build each section of the book around the concept of what the research tells us, why it is essential, and how you can apply it. I strive to achieve a balance between giving enough information to convince you of its value, but not so much you feel overwhelmed.

It is important to remember the brain is by nature suspicious and distrusting. Your brain has a natural tendency to say "I don't believe this. Show me the evidence." To counter this, I will refer to the research and will provide links to what is original research.

I will present my interpretation of the research and the insights on how to use it to develop yourself. My view is filtered through my brain, my experiences, and is unique to me. You may find you disagree with some of my opinions, and that's alright. The references to the research are there, and I encourage you to appease your brain's skepticism by reading them and developing your own opinions. I hope they mesh with mine, but if they don't, I believe you will still find it valuable and be able to use it.

Brainsights also has a companion website where you can ask questions, discuss, and debate the research and the ideas presented in the book. It is a forum to extend the book, and I welcome you to join us on Facebook at:

https://www.facebook.com/BrainsightsBook

INTRODUCTION

Brainsights is the result of years of research into neuroscience and how to apply it. The motivation has been to provide my clients with a better understanding of their behavior and others. Understanding what drives behavior is important to working and living better.

For the last 20 years, I have been coaching people in leadership and sales in multinational companies. I have been fortunate to work around the world with people from over 70 countries, on four continents, from many organizations. The focus of my work has been on providing insight into what drives our own behavior and the behavior of others and how that knowledge can be used to bring about positive change.

I first encountered neuroscience back in 2008 when I was working on building a personality profiling app for sales professionals. Knowing humans are always looking for the shortest path to success, I worried the process I developed for determining a person's personality was too complicated. There were just ten questions, but the human brain is so resistant to complex tasks, which I'll get into later in the book. I wondered if there is an easier way to reveal a person's personality. Ideally, I would have liked to turn a phone on and to have it determine it.

After a few days of searching on Google, I found out this was possible. What's more is that a team of researchers in Germany and Israel had been researching and developing predictive algorithms along the same lines. The research used fMRI machines to analyzed tone and timbre to predict how the listener would interpret a vocal message (Simon-Thomas, et al. 2009) (Oberman and Pineda 2007).

The researchers tested over 1 million messages on subjects in fMRI machines mapping the areas of the brain triggered by vocal timbres. The correlation between the timbres and specific attitudes were extrapolated, and an algorithm was created to determine in real-time how well a person's message was being accepted.

In its implemented state the system did not extract personality, but it was possible. Ultimately, I decided not to incorporate the technology into my app. It was too far ahead of its time, and I worried about the implications of auto-determining people's personalities and then using this information to sell (interestingly, several years after my search for a way to auto determine personality, a company called Crystal Knows is doing this trough analysis of social media). However, it opened my eyes and gave me insight into the world of neuroscience and the possibilities for understanding people and their behavior from a science-based perspective.

This scientific explanation of people's behavior presented me with a compelling tool I could use in my leadership and sales coaching and training work. My clients were multinational B2B organizations with engineering mindsets who were by nature data-driven people.

In the 20 years I have been in this business, one of the main challenges I've encountered is the skepticism people have towards 'soft skills', the people skills which are apparently important to success. Many of my clients wanted to see hard data showing the correlation between people skills and performance.

Neuroscience research provided the data and served as a foundation for a better understanding of human behavior. The data showed how behavior resulted from our brain's process of stimulus. Understand the process better, and you could positively impact your performance and others.

By incorporating neuroscience into my coaching and training programs, I provided the hard data the skeptics needed to convince them soft skills were important to success. They could see research confirming specific actions, words, and mannerisms resulted in specific chemical reactions in others. Those chemical reactions, known as neurotransmitters, triggered areas of the brain responsible for behavior.

Historically, research into behavior was the exclusive discipline of psychology. My first experience with designing training programs relied on research coming from psychology. The primary influence for me was work carried out by the U.S. military on best practices for developing leaders using a process called artificial experience building, an experiential form of learning. I continue to use this method today, but now augment it with supporting data from neuroscience to provide further proof of effectiveness.

The disadvantage of psychology compared to neuroscience is that psychology is rooted in observed behavior and observations are open to interpretation. Neuroscience, on the other hand, looks at blood flow in the brain and neural activity. For example, neuroscience can tell us the same area of the brain is activated when we hear language or music, suggesting a link between the two.

In the last ten years, the number of researchers in neuroscience has skyrocketed to more than 50 000. Neuroscience is excellent for understanding observed psychological phenomena regarding root processes and mechanisms and is now at a stage where it can predict real-world outcomes (Berkman and Falk 2013). I am not arguing neuroscience should replace psychology. Behavior is complex, and it would be impossible to study it by using neuroscience alone. But neuroscience can, and does, build on psychology to provide further proof of our observations.

The foundation of a better understanding of ourselves and others is to understand how evolution, biology, and experience work together to shape our views and actions.

We are entering a wondrous time of exploration and discovery leading us to an evolved understanding of ourselves and others. I hope this book opens a door to knowledge helpful to you in building an exceptional life.

YOUR BRAIN PREFERS TO THINK IT IS 4000 B.C.

Two systems make up your brain

Nobel Prize-winning economist Daniel Kahneman created one of the most straightforward explanations of how your brain works – an explanation that is both easy to remember and perfect for helping you to get a birds-eye view of the distinct areas of our brains and their functions.

In his book, *Thinking Fast and Slow* (Kahneman 2011), Kahneman describes the brain as working in two systems which he terms System 1 (S1) and System 2 (S2). System 1 is all about instinct and survival and System 2 is about logic and reasoning. Every day, you use both systems to navigate the complexity of your environment with the primary goal being to avoid threat and maximize reward. I will borrow the terminology of S1 and S2 from Kahneman to refer to these two brain systems throughout the book to help keep things simple.

Your Lizard Brain (S1)

The S1 brain is your intuitive and instinctual brain. It is responsible for the 4 Fs of survival: Feeding, Fighting, Fleeing and Fornication. It is most commonly referred to as the reptilian or lizard brain*. This part of our brain developed long before the other parts.

*Side note: Although we like to casually refer to our S1 brain as the 'lizard brain', it has not evolved from reptiles. The term is only a descriptive way for us to refer to the primitive part of our brains. Some, most famously the astronomer Carl Sagan, might have liked to think this ancient part of our brain could have evolved from reptiles, and the 'newer' areas of our brains developed on top of the older ones. While this idea has been a part of popular belief for decades, it isn't supported by neuroscience.

When referring to the brain in his work, even Carl Sagan was careful to note that the models were 'oversimplifications' and represented nothing more than a 'metaphor of great utility and depth'.

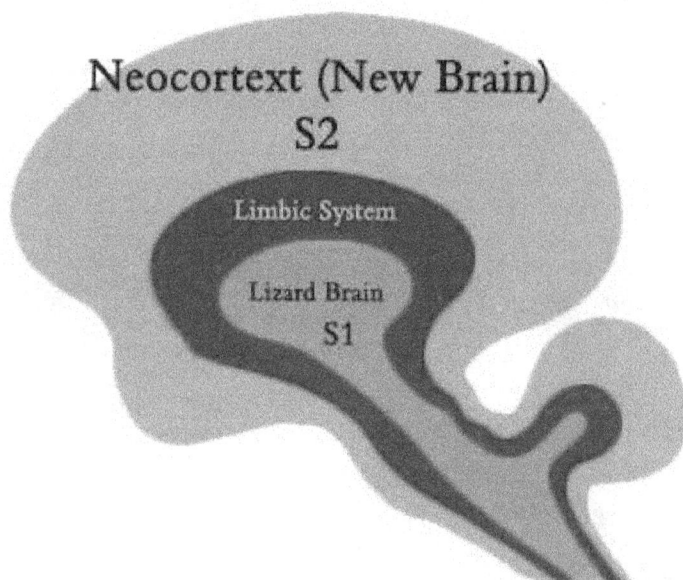

Neuroscientists believe new brain structures are modified versions of old brain structures. This is what I will set as the foundation of our discussion of the brain structure. I will refer to the 'oversimplified' explanations of the brain as a starting point for discussions and not as an absolute truth of science. As the physicist Emerson M Pugh once said: "If the brain were simple enough for us to understand it, we would be so simple that we couldn't." If we are to get to what is useful for us to understand, we cannot get caught in the web of complexity.

S1 is always on alert scanning our environment every 1/5th of a second looking for threats. Our lizard brains are even active in searching for hazards when we are asleep. I'm sure some of you have been woken up by your brain in the middle of a deep sleep because a noise, or some event, has alerted you that something's not right. This is your S1 brain at work.

It handles about 95% of what we do on a day-to-day basis. It is your unconscious brain, responsible for essential body functions and accountable for things like walking, talking and language. It also has a built-in negativity bias designed to exaggerate fears and increase anxiety with the mission to protect at all costs.

When your lizard brain (S1) perceives a threat, it reacts instantaneously. In the animal and early humanoid world of the past, those who reacted faster were more likely to survive. The lizard brain made the decision as quickly as possible (about a fifth of a second (Libet, et al. 1983) from a rapid, subconscious processing of information collected from our senses. The animal brain does not test risk and decide on actions; it only senses danger and acts.

Skip ahead to the present day and ask yourself: does the need for such a system still make sense? It does not. Few of us live in a survival-based environment where speed of reaction determines if we live or die. But many of your day-to-day behaviors are driven by your lizard brain's desire to make instantaneous decisions.

When faced with a threat you can feel your lizard brain dump a cocktail of hormones into your body to hijack your thoughts and direct your behavior towards rushed, often ill-thought, actions.

Our brains have evolved little beyond the need to survive, and this is important to remember and recognize in yourself and others. We prefer to react and want to respond to a stimulus without using our higher order system two (S2) brain.

Your Logical Brain (S2)

The S2 brain is your new brain, the brain responsible for deliberate, focused analytical brain activity and demanding physical tasks.

Examples of S2 brain activity include analyzing data, complex computations, checking if an argument is logical and even things such as looking for a red-haired woman in a crowded room and comparing products. Most importantly, your S2 brain is responsible for exercising self-control.

Your brain weighs only 1/12th of your body, but it consumes a whopping 20% of your energy (Raichle and Gusnard 2002). When you use your S2 brain, it puts energy use into high mode and is consuming calories at a rapid rate. Have you ever noticed when you are working on a demanding task, such as studying for an exam, writing a project debrief, or preparing for an outstanding presentation, you get an overwhelming desire for sugar? This is your S2 brain consuming energy and demanding you give it more. As you become more skilled at a task the S2 brain works to move it down to the S1, to an automatic process, which is more energy efficient.

Side note: There has been some debate in recent years about whether brain activity decreases the availability of glucose to the body. However, a 2018 review of the body of evidence from the field of brain metabolism concluded that 'glucose levels within specific brain areas can be acutely decreased by cognitive demand calling on those areas, and that such drainage places a limit on cognitive processing' (Benjamin C. Ampel 2018).

Something that is important to know about our S2 brain is that it limits focus. It cannot calculate math problems, do a difficult physical activity, or look for patterns in a group all at the same time. Nor is it possible to move straight from one demanding task to another without time to rest and recover.

Your brain is a crystal ball

It seems that the human mind has first to construct forms independently before we can find them in things.

Albert Einstein

Your brain is predictive and not reactive. Einstein was correct in his observation that the brain first needs to construct forms to realize them in the physical world. The world is chaotic and ever-changing, bombarding us with a continuum of sensations. If your brain was not predictive, it would be overwhelmed with trying to make sense of all this information.

The brain constantly takes input from the environment and compares it to past experiences stored in memory to predict what is likely to be experienced next. It sends information back to the sensory regions of our brain and compares the predictions to the data it is receiving. It then disregards most, if not all, the data not matching with the expected prediction. Understandably, the mismatch between what is predicted and what is experienced results in errors. Your brain's desperate desire to make predictions for every situation prevents you from looking objectively at anything.

Sports provides a simple understanding of your predictive brain. If your brain was reactive, it would not be fast enough to process the stream of input necessary to be able to block a shot or hit a ball, to do this we need to be predictive.

For example, when Roger Federer returns a serve he must predict where the ball will go and react to move his body into position. What is amazing is it is not his eye directing his body, but his brain. The eye is too slow and the lag would make it impossible for him to be in the right position to successfully return a serve. Instead the brain calculates the eye lag and tells it where to move to return the serve (Elle van Heusden 2018). The predictive ability gets better with practice and top athletes do have better abilities in this area than the average person.

If you were purely reactive, you would be in a constant state of surprise. No matter what you experience, your brain would be amazed, having no idea it was going to happen. Your brain would also be very slow as all information would need to be processed and a course of action determined beforehand.

Most children can quite easily catch a ball thrown to them, but it's difficult to build a robot that can catch a ball. Why? Because the robot lacks our rapid predictive abilities. It cannot quickly and reliably predict what is going to happen when someone throws a ball at it. It lacks the ability to process the situation and make the best guess of where it is going to go and direct itself into proper position to catch it. The child's brain, on the other hand, can and does do this with remarkable accuracy.

Neuroscience has brought increasingly relevant findings to this 'intuitive' ability of the brain. There is a growing consensus that predictions about the future are realized in the brain by a complex hierarchy of neural process working together to continually update how we view our world (S. Chennu 2013).

One experiment from Radboud University in the Netherlands was able to show the predictive nature of the brain. Using fMRI scanning of the brain, researchers had participants view movies of a white dot moving across a screen. After 108 viewings, it was found participants developed a mental expectation of the dot's movement. Researchers then had them watched movies where the dot moved in unexpected ways. What the brain scans revealed was the participant's brain completed the movement of the dot in the manner expected from the first 108 viewings.

Not only was the brain completing the movements for them, but it was being completed twice as fast as it occurred (Matthias Ekman 2017). It normally took one second for the dot to move across the screen in the original movies, but the fMRI scans showed the brain was completing the movement in less than half a second. People didn't need to process the visual input to know where the dot was going, they knew where it was going. It didn't matter if new information was telling them differently, their brains disregarded it and completed the movement as expected.

Researchers caution this is a simplified example compared to what we experience in real life, but it does show the brain predicts the future. Interestingly, this research also found that prediction is independent of consciousness, suggesting it is an automated process (Matthias Ekman 2017).

Think about how much of your everyday life is reliant on automated prediction. From anticipating tennis balls coming at us and positioning ourselves to hit it, to observing a dog running out in front of our car and swerving to miss it, to the simple act of walking down the street and putting one foot in front of another. Without prediction, even simple things in life would be impossible.

But it also keeps us from fully comprehending and taking advantage of new experiences. We want to quickly, without higher-order S2 thought, categorize everything as something we know and recognize and have experienced before, when the truth is it simply may not be.

The famous magician Teller (of Penn and Teller), participated in a study with researchers at the Barrow Neurological Institute in Phoenix, Arizona, to investigate the human mind and its ability to build false perceptions. What Teller (his full legal name) was able to show researchers is how magic exploits the human mind to fill in gaps in information to see what we predict we will see. Pulling a rabbit out of a hat, making a coin disappear, even sawing a woman in half, are all demonstrations of your brain's wish to skip ahead and see what it wants to see and ignore what does not fit with expectations. Many magic tricks are good examples of your brain at work, and neuroscientists are taking magic into the lab to study how the brain reacts to them (Macknik, et al. n.d.).

Each of us sees what we want to see. This tendency is the source of conflict and pain in our lives. Your brain feeds you select information, the minimum it needs to make a reasonable guess to what is going on. This 'reasonable guess' is what keeps you from fully exploring new ideas, opinions, and perspectives. Your brain's desire to be efficient conspires against you, preventing you from being creative, innovative, and respectful of other people's ideas. Learning to reexamine situations to incorporate new information is how to open yourself to new possibilities and not become a victim of your own brain.

Neuroscientist Beau Lotto explains:

"People have this assumption that if they don't see the world objectively, it'll create chaos. But by not seeing the world objectively, it creates possibility. It creates freedom. Accuracy is not the same thing as utility: I might see a rock accurately but seeing it accurately doesn't tell me what to do with it. If one of our ancestors saw a rock, they could have seen it with possibility and opportunity and shaped it to become a tool. Our brain evolved to take what is meaningless and make it meaningful, what's useless and make it useful." (Lotto 2017)

Once you understand the uniqueness of your view and the view of others, you can embrace it and celebrate it. Know your brain is going to fight looking at things differently. How to get beyond this limitation is to force your S2 brain to be unsatisfied with the first answer but to push for the next right answer. In the process you open yourself up to unlimited possibilities.

S1 prioritizes emotion over logic

Evolution has played a part in shaping how our S2 brain works and its connection to our S1 brains. The brain is energy-intensive and hungry for calories to feed its operation. To maximize survival, the brain has evolved to prioritize functions determined to be vital to sustaining life. Those functions – breathing, heartbeat, blood flow, all your critical body functions – along with threat detection are the domain of S1 and it has priority.

All higher-order thinking is automatically shut down whenever the brain determines it is unnecessary. And even when it is necessary, it still may not be given the energy to operate if your S1 brain determines there is a risk you will not run short of energy for critical bodily functions.

It took humanity 2.5 million years to get out of the Stone Age because the human brain lacked the excess energy to fuel our high-order thinking. We looked for every occasion to conserve energy. We took every shortcut we could and relied on what we knew already worked. It was not until systematic agriculture, about 12 000 years ago, which allowed humanity to have enough spare calories to use more of our S2 brain functions, enabling an increase in creativity and problem solving.

Our world has changed, but our brains have not

It is important to remember that, even though our world has changed, our brains still function as though we were living 10 000 years ago. This insight above all else can help you understand better yourself and others. Let's look at a few examples and suggestions on how to use our newfound awareness.

S1 is all about the automatic. It is habit-based, instantaneous, and prefers to get from point A to point B quickly and with as little effort as possible.

You like to trust your raw emotions because they help you make quick decisions, ones not requiring energy to contemplate alternatives. Your emotions are a reaction to chemicals released by your brain that encourages you to act on impulse. We often refer to this as our 'gut' feeling or 'intuition', and this is what it is.

Side note: Emotions and feelings are not the same thing. We often use them interchangeably but there is a distinction between the two. Emotions are signals from the body. For example, the emotion of anxiety is manifested in our body by heart palpitations, perspiration, shortness of breath, insomnia, restlessness. Emotion is well known to affect basic brain functions such as attention, memory, vision and motor control. Feeling is then the conscious realization of what our body is telling us. Therefore, emotions are our initial stance towards reality and feelings are our long-term view of reality. We cannot have feelings without the emotions that triggered our conscious thinking.

100-millisecond judgments

With people, we use this intuition in as little as 100 milliseconds to form an opinion (Janine Willis, Alexander Todorov 2006). Researchers at Princeton University conducted five experiments each focusing on a specific trait of judgments such as attractiveness, likability, trustworthiness, competence, and aggressiveness. It took just 100 milliseconds for people to formulate judgments. Notably, those initial judgments did not change if given more time to evaluate.

In another study published in the Journal of Neuroscience and conducted at New York University's Department of Psychology, researchers found the brain automatically responds to a face's trustworthiness before being consciously perceived (Freeman, et al. 2014). Our subconscious forms an opinion before we know our brain has decided on how we view this person.

We judge a person's faces in milliseconds

The brain is filtering the stimulus we get – in this case, a person's face – through our past experiences and trying to connect it with existing memories to draw conclusions. The implications are our brains prevent us from seeing any person, or situation, objectively. Everything we experience runs through the filter of our memory. From here, we try to make a connection to help us comprehend who or what we are seeing.

Charles Darwin was one of the first to theorize there is a universal expression of emotion across cultures visible in our facial expressions. The inspiration for his theory was his travels on the HMS Beagle. The story is Darwin found that no matter where he went, even if there was no common language, it was possible to communicate through a shared understanding of emotion. He concluded emotional expressions are evolved traits universal to the human species and not learned. He published his findings in the book, *The Expression of the Emotions in Man and Animals,* published in 1872. (Darwin 1872).We all express emotions the same way – through our facial expressions. This provides humans with an ability to understand the emotions of others and react to them, giving us an evolutionary advantage.

In the 70s, American Psychologist Paul Ekman built on the work of Darwin developing techniques for measuring nonverbal communication, focusing on facial movements. Ekman spent decades researching the expression of emotions across cultures through the face. As Darwin did, Ekman concluded emotions are expressed universally. He settled on 7 expressions of emotion: disgust, anger, fear, sadness, happiness, contempt, and surprise (Paul Ekman 1971).

However, neuroscientist Lisa Feldman Barrett has reopened the debate around the universal expression of emotion. She researched emotion looking for the 'fingerprint' of where emotions are stored in the brain. But instead of finding a fingerprint, her research led to the conclusion there is not one area in the brain that manages individual emotions like anger, but all emotion is constructed and those constructions rarely match with reality.

According to Barrett, humans are bad at interpreting facial expressions as signals of emotion, and there is no direct evidence the body is producing physical manifestations of emotion. Her own research, and a meta-analysis of hundreds of other studies, showed so much depends on context and circumstance and too often we are influenced by our expectations (Barrett 2017).

Tsarnaev's stoic stare

In a 2016 TED Talk. Barrett speaks about convicted Boston marathon bomber Dzhokhar Tsarnaev who the jury sentenced to death. The criteria for deciding if a person should receive the death penalty or life imprisonment is the level of remorse the person demonstrates. In Tsarnaev's case when he gave his statement before sentencing, jurors described him as having a 'blank stare' which many interpreted as a lack of remorse, and this cost him his life. But Barrett argues that what others viewed as a lack of remorse was just his way of stoically accepting defeat, which is his culture's (Chechen) way of accepting it (Barrett, You aren't at the mercy of your emotions – your brain creates them 2017).

The danger is you can get it wrong when it comes to the judgments your brain makes in milliseconds. People are not proficient at interpreting emotions in others. The brain's preference for not using our executive functions (S2) for further analysis and validation, results in grossly incorrect interpretations of situations and people.

In my work with clients I have used the work of Paul Ekman and his universal emotions in leadership and sales programs. One of the reasons for using it was to focus people's attention on others when interacting with them, whether that be in providing feedback to a report, or in delivering a sales presentation. Too often we fail to pay attention to what people are expressing with their bodies and miss the clues to how they are taking what we are presenting. By teaching the 7 universal emotions to people and providing an opportunity to practice reading those emotions from people's faces, it forced participants to move the processing of faces from an automatic process by their S1 brain, to their S2 high-order processing. They had to observe and think about what the person's face tells them.

In working with hundreds of people from a wide variety of cultures I found that some could identify emotions with ease, and with others it took training. It was clear there were people who had an innate ability to correctly identify facial expressions and connect them to emotions, even when only flashed for a microsecond on a computer screen.

What I believe, and have experienced, is our faces reveal our emotions. Do we get it wrong? Yes we do – and often. The reason we get it wrong is our rush to judgment, believing we see something our brains have been primed to see.

Barret is right in her conclusions: we like to construct what we believe we should be seeing or have been primed to see. It is far easier, and less energy-intensive, than sustaining focus and suspending judgment until we have a more accurate picture. Boston bomber Tsarnaev was seen as an 'evil' character for most people, including the jurors at his trial. They expected to see he was unremorseful and this primed their brains to see that and deliver a death sentence.

What is important to take away from this discussion is the importance of suspending judgment. Keep from falling into your S1's trap of seeing what you expect to see and acting only on it. You can move away from incorrect millisecond judgments by recognizing when your brain is making a snap judgment and forcing it to revisit and revise.

Everyone has an individual view of the world

Dr. Anil Seth from the University of Sussex in the UK is a neuroscientist researching perception and the brain. His research has brought to light how the brain makes assumptions based on interpretations and experiences. Seth's research focused on the brain's interpretation of color, finding it is individual.

Have you ever argued with someone about the color of something? My wife and I frequently get into heated arguments about the color of a shirt, sweater, or jacket. She would insist it was one color, me another, with both of us unable to understand how the other could not see the 'real color'. According to Seth, it is not because we are color blind (as my wife tried to insist, I was), but because of our brain's individual and unique interpretation of color.

One example of the brain's interpretation of color is a well-known Internet social phenomenon from 2015 known simply as 'the dress'. An impassioned debate ensued about the color of a cocktail dress posted in the social media platform Tumblr. The dress, pictured below, generated over 73 million views in a matter of days. Was it gold and white or black and blue? Which do you see? (The Dress 2018)

The Dress 2015 - Swiked/Tumblr

I was skeptical when I first heard about 'the dress' I wondered, "Can this be true? Is there a visible difference in what people see?" There is no doubt in my mind I see the dress as gold and white. When I asked my son to tell me what color the dress was, with no other explanation, he replied, "It's blue and black." Not only were the colors different, but they were as different as black and white. I was stunned.

The explanation lies in the research Dr. Seth carried out on color. He explains the dress is a perfect example of how we each have been programmed to see the world in distinct ways. For our brains, the stimulus we get is only ambiguous electrical signals that require processing to make sense. We do this through probabilistic inference where we try to match a new stimulus with prior expectations of what we think it could be (Seth 2018).

Our brain combines those prior expectations with signals coming from the outside world to create a 'best guess' of what it's encountering. The brain is constantly at work, desperate to make sense of the noisy and ambiguous flood of sensory information coming in.

The reality is the dress is not white and gold, but blue and black. If you are like me and see the dress as white and gold it is because we view the world in natural sunlight, while the black and blue people think the artificial indoor light is illuminating it (Seth 2018). The theory is those who see white and gold have a 'sunnier' outlook on life, more positive.

Seth's research is an important reminder that you have an individual interpretation of the world. It's dangerous to assume others always see the world as you do, and we should constantly try to avoid making this assumption.

We also know from neuroscience there is six times more information flowing back from our thalamus (which is responsible for sensory interpretation) as we work to make sense of visual information coming in. It is proof of your brain hard at work to make sense of the visual stimuli you are receiving. It is not 'recording' what you see and playing it back in your head. Instead, it is taking in the information and using rapid processing to see if it corresponds with something you already know. To do this it has to recreate the neural connections that created the memory. If it finds a relationship that makes sense, it associates the new stimulus and updates the context.

Priming the brain for experience

Another way to understand in practice how the brain interprets and connects to existing stored memory is by looking at our eyes. Our eyes are in continuous motion, moving on average 100 000 times a day, over 3 times a second. If we wire a video camera to record video according to our eye movement, the result would be a jumpy, blurry, and impossible-to-watch mess. Why then is your sight not a mess? It is because you use the information already in your brain to create most of the scene, only updating it with what is determined to be new from incoming stimuli not matched to your stored memories (Rolfs, et al. 2011).

If you take a coin in your fingers and stretch your arms out in front of you and focus your eye on the coin, this is near to the range your eyes take in information. Notice how when you focus on that point, all other information blurs and is imperceptible.

Want to test your brain and see how this works? You can recreate the famous eye movement experiment by Russian psychologist Alfred Lukyanovich Yarbus from 1967. He had people look at a painting and then asked questions about its contents. To simulate this experiment, stop reading and look at the picture below entitled 'The Unexpected Visitor'.

Ilya Repin in 1884 - Public Domain

Now hide the image and answer the following question:

How many pictures are on the wall?

Now look back at the picture. Were you right? I am sure you got it very wrong. Why? Because your brain was not primed to look for that information. You were primed to look at the people in the painting. The title 'The Unexpected Visitor' primed your brain and focused your eye movements on the people in the room and what they are doing.

Yarbus observed the same when he tracked people's eyes. Depending on how he primed participants their eye movements varied. The brain does not process all the information coming in. It must select a focus and direct your attention to that focus to keep from being overwhelmed. But this means we also don't see things as they are, but as our brain expects them to be or as we believe they should be (Data Deluge, 2012).

As philosopher Herman Helmholtz said, "We remember what we perceive, and we perceive – intuitively or unconsciously – what we remember."

Culture embeds experience

Think of the implications for your life when considering how your brain filters and disregards. Upbringing, culture, education: the whole gamut of experiences filters how you see things. It is not surprising multinational organizations have a hard time getting people to see the business in the same way.

I have struggled with this for the last 20 years as an expat living in Finland and the Czech Republic. I often ask, "Why on earth is this done that way here? It makes no sense." But the things that make little sense to me make perfect sense to those whose experience and upbringing differs from mine.

An excellent example of this came when I was giving a lecture on leadership to a group of young business students. Part of my presentation was showing pictures painted by leaders from a training program for a multinational. One painting, depicted by an Italian man, showed himself standing behind his team as they climbed a mountain. His idea was a leader always stands behind and supports his team. However, a young Finnish male business student, Karl, had a different interpretation.

Karl stopped me in the middle of my presentation and asked how that picture represented good leadership. He explained that a leader leads from the front. and proceeded to tell of how Russian commanders in World War II stood behind the conscripts and shot any who refused to fight.

Karl had just completed his mandatory military service, and it was easy to see what was driving his interpretation. It was well-reported the Russians forced their conscripts to fight and had orders from Lenin to shoot any who refused. For this young Finnish man, the image of standing behind your team only brought up stories of Russian commanders in World War II.

It is not that one person who had a better interpretation of leadership than the other – each had a valid way of looking at it. However, the expression of the concept was different because it was shaped by their individual experience.

What if Karl had an Italian boss who explained this leadership philosophy' to him? How do you think he would view his boss? Do you understand the difficulties and why we struggle to work across cultures? Let me provide another example highlighting the business costs.

A multinational client I worked for in 2008 had undertaken to open a new factory in mainland China for manufacturing their industrial products. They cloned the manufacturing plant they had in Northern Europe, known for producing high-quality products. They built the factory and started manufacturing. From the first month of production, quality problems appeared at an alarming rate. Surprised and perplexed, they could not understand how this plant could have such a drastically inferior quality to the plant in Europe. The processes and workflow were identical.

The problem was not in the factory design but in the minds of those who worked there. It was explained to me a couple of years later by a Chinese manager from the same company who was a participant in my leadership training program. He explained, for the Chinese, quality is not about over-engineering a product, which is seen as a waste of time and money. Products should meet the minimum level needed for their function and nothing more. It was how their brains, filtered through their experience and reinforced by their culture, told them to define and interpret quality.

For the company, it meant educating to 'rewire' the brains of the Chinese workers to create a new interpretation of quality, one matching the expectations of their customers.

Training yourself to be situationally aware

The examples above all seem obvious in hindsight but when in the situation it is more difficult to understand the forces at work preventing you from success. This is why it is necessary to train your brain to have a heightened awareness of your surroundings and the environment, a skill which is called 'situational awareness.' Through a heightened sense of awareness, your brain takes another look at the information it's receiving and reprocesses it to plan an alternate, more accurate, prediction of the future.

The term situational awareness originated in combat aviation as one of the decisive factors to a positive outcome for World War I pilots (Watts, 1996). The elements of situational awareness are comprised of perception, comprehension, and projection. Together these three factors provide us with a full view of situations and guide us in better decision making.

Perception and comprehension are how we notice the environment and understand the information coming into our brains. To fully know the situation, it is essential to have high familiarity with the system you are using, put aside assumptions, and keep your mind alert to changes.

To get to this level of understanding, you must fight your brain which is trying to take shortcuts and apply mental rules that don't always provide you with an accurate, or current picture of what you are experiencing.

The third part, projection, is the ability to project into the future what will happen based on an assessment of the information received. It allows you to anticipate the future and apply reason to direct your actions towards outcomes having a higher rate of success.

To become more situationally aware, you need to train and build your experience. You cannot expect to develop your mind to the level of sophistication necessary to understand your limitations, or how to bypass them, without building your database of experience.

It takes a minimum of 2 760 hours of training before a military pilot gets into the cockpit of a fighter plane and another 1 to 2 years of intense training before they are competent enough to engage in combat. It is a lot of hours, most spent in simulation, building 'artificial experience'.

Just as a fighter pilot must train to develop their skills to a level where they can direct a strike force, destroy enemy radar, monitor surface-to-air missiles and track enemy aircraft all while flying at 700 feet per second, you need to train your own situational awareness abilities to function at a higher level. You have two choices for developing those abilities: one, you can learn by doing on the job, or two, you can build experience artificially.

The problem with learning while doing, is you are often subjected to several failures in pursuit of experience which is costly and often painful. To use our example, a fighter pilot crashing an F-18 Hornet would be hugely expensive –about $70 million – and life-threatening. Using artificial experience, you can develop skills without the associated costs or risks.

Artificial experience builds situational awareness

I have been using artificial experience to build the experience base of people in my programs for over 20 years to help them develop better situational awareness.

The background to the method I developed for my programs came from the US military. When I was just out of college in 1988, I moved to Washington D.C. and worked at the National Archives and Records Administration of the United States in records declassification. I spent my days reading top-secret classified materials and deciding if I could recommend them for declassification. I came across a method for training battlefield commanders called 'artificial experience building'. The foundation for the training still used today is David A. Kolb's experiential learning model (ELM) which Kolb developed in 1984 (Kolb 1984).

Military commanders took part in elaborate battlefield simulations requiring them to make what were often life and death decisions, building new experiences in the brain. Dr. David Pierson, in the Journal of Military Learning, explains the process:

"The concrete experience introduces a new experience or reinterprets an existing one. During reflective observation, the learners consider similarities and differences between the new experience and their own experiences. In abstract conceptualization, the learners form concepts, analyze them, and form general conclusions related to these concepts; they learn from the experience. Finally, during active experimentation, the learners apply their conclusions to a different situation creating a new experience. By touching on all four of the stages of the learning cycle, learners construct knowledge by experiencing, reflecting, thinking, and acting." (Pierson 2017)

The military psychologists determined this was an effective method for building combat experience in a safe environment. Research continues to support artificial experience being as valid as real-life experience and is effective (Gosen and Washbush 2004). Therefore, when we have new experiences, even if they are artificial, the brain will use this new embedded knowledge to test new information, helping to build greater situational awareness.

I use roleplay to create characters and situations steeped in emotion and unexpected challenges, raising the stress level and activating, to a degree, the flight or fight stressors that lead to poor decisions. After they have completed the roleplay, we take time to assess the approach to the situation and alternatives. We then allow the person to 'replay' the experience incorporating the feedback, which allows them to internalize the new experience.

Let me describe an example from one of my training programs to demonstrate how this works. I was running an artificial experience building program for a scientific instrument company in leadership. One participant, Kathy (not her real name), came with a case of how to manage her boss.

Kathy was the VP of marketing and part of a group of eight persons making up the organization's management team. Each month the management team met for a status update. The problem Kathy had was in every status meeting she was scheduled to deliver her report last. As happens in many multi-reporting meetings, people go over their allotted time. At every status update, Kathy found herself with half the time she should have had and rushing through her presentation. She felt the situation was unfair and wanted to discuss this with her boss with me playing the boss.

I spent a few moments with Kathy to understand the personality of her boss, and she described a headstrong, dominant male – an easy role for me to play.

The first iteration of the case, we jumped in and started to role-play it. Kathy came to the simulated office and opened the discussion explaining how it was unfair she had to present last at every meeting and then asked, "Is there something you don't like about me? Is there some reason you think I should not be allowed to give my whole presentation to the team?" We continued to role-play for a few moments, with me denying it had anything to do with her personally, stating she was overreacting, and to not worry about it. I concluded by saying that I thought she usually had enough time, but I promised to watch the time better. It was a harsh dismissal of her, and one likely to occur in real life. I then put the case on pause and we pulled apart her approach.

As we talked through her tactics, it became clear Kathy was insecure about her abilities, and this led her to believe her boss also lacked confidence in her. She had assessed the situation, and her brain had jumped to the emotional conclusion that she went last because her boss didn't want her to present.

By stepping back and considering the situation and the personality of her boss, I helped her realize her approach would not get her the result she wanted, which was her presentation slot changed. The boss, being a dominant personality type, probably would not respond favorably to appeals to his sense of fairness or to the implication he doesn't like her or trust her abilities. In fact, it could make the situation worse by planting a seed of doubt in his mind, and thus reducing his confidence in her.

It is a misconception dominant people are entirely self-reliant. In a 2014 neuroscience study by researchers at Radboud University found that dominant people pay close attention and learn from people who they identify as successful. Using this insight to guide their behavior for personal gain. Researchers concluded "socially dominant people explicitly value independence but show an enhanced reliance, relative to subordinate individuals, on social learning when in a complex decision-making situation," (Cook, et al. 2014). If you want to influence a dominant personality type, one tactic is to appeal to their social-learning needs. Show them you have something they can learn from and will help them to be more successful.

Together Kathy and I constructed another approach based on heightened perception and comprehension of the situation, the goal being to project a future that delivered the result Kathy wanted.

Kathy mapped out a case for how not being able to present her entire status report was a risk for the organization and for him personally. She identified a few examples which illustrated her point, showing how a lack of understanding could potentially lead to dangerous misunderstandings. She then took a dominant approach (matching his dominance) and demanded in the next group meeting to report first.

Replaying this second approach it was clear both to Kathy and me this would be better received. I found it difficult to argue her position should not be changed, which is always a clear indication the approach is a better one.

I followed up with Kathy a few months later to see if she used the new strategy and if it worked. Not surprisingly, it did, and her report position changed. It also boosted her confidence in her own abilities to use situational awareness and experience to orchestrate successful outcomes.

Artificial experience has proven to be a valuable tool to change our perception of a situation and provide a higher level of situational awareness. It updates our own personal experience database which provides more information for analysis and increases the possibility of comprehending more. With better comprehension comes an ability to project a future with outcomes that support what you desire. And when you can project your future with greater confidence you can direct your behavior and take actions to realize a better future.

Artificial experience building is not just for military or corporate training, you can accomplish it on a smaller scale. Roleplay is valuable in a wide spectrum of situations, from work-related to personal. If you can assign characters and behaviors to individuals to roleplay, then you can create a valuable experience. Don't limit using this tool to your work life – it can also be very effective in your personal life, helping you to understand alternative perspectives and develop new courses of action to deal with challenges.

I often coach people in organizations to use the artificial experience building techniques they encounter in my training programs with trusted colleagues, friends, and even spouses. Our brains have a remarkable ability to create realism out of artificially created situations. As long as the person roleplaying with you takes it seriously, and does the utmost to play the situation honestly, it will be beneficial.

Here are a few tips for effective Artificial Experience Building role-play.

1. Set a time limit for the role-play. I use between 7- and 12-minutes max. If you get to the core of what the problem is, this is plenty of time.
2. Discuss the character you are meeting. Know who it is you are meeting from a personality perspective. What type of person are they? How are they likely to act in the situation? You are taking liberties in guessing their reaction, but remember it is about building experience, and any reaction played will be valuable in creating experience.
3. Have your role-play partner construct an emotional starting point. I suggest the following: angry, sad, disappointed, indifferent, or annoyed. Be sure the role-player does not share their starting point with you. By keeping it a surprise, it will be more realistic. After all, we rarely know how someone will react in real life situations.
4. Role-play from the problem point. Don't spend a lot of time role-playing introductions and everyday niceties, get to the meat of the problem.
5. It is okay if they overact it. Don't worry about being 100% realistic. I have found often the greatest insight into a problem comes from role-playing an extreme version. The experience, even an extreme one, forces the brain to build a new model.

6. Stop the role-play and explore other options for approaching the problem if it does not feel right or is going in a direction that is not productive. If it does not feel right, then you have not found yet the insight you need. Stop and take a moment to examine what is happening. Why doesn't it feel right? What else could change the path the discussion is taking? Discuss and try again with a new approach.

7. Don't just discuss the solutions, but role-play then. For the brain, discussion alone does not connect. To internalize what you have learned, it is important to feel how it works by role-playing it again. This also gives you the opportunity to test your new hypothesis about how to handle the situation and see if it works.

8. Last, spend the time to review and be self-critical. Part of being situationally aware is being able to be critical of your own actions. Are you filtering the situation too much, if so, what can you do to force your brain to reprocess?

In the next section we will look at how experience is committed to memory.

Understanding our memory

Why is it you can remember the neighbor's dog likes to bite, but you cannot remember his wife's name? It is a matter of priority and survival. A dog who bites is a threat to our well-being while the name of our neighbor's wife, not so important to remember – unless she is a dangerous woman. One ensures your safety while the other is just a piece of random information – or as scientists like to refer to it, neutral information.

Our memories are bewildering, complex, and frustrating. A good metaphor for memory is wet paint. Before paint has dried and set, it is vulnerable to disturbance. The slightest touch can alter it and with not too much more effort it can be wiped away entirely.

Memories are the same way. Before we have moved them to long-term memory (LTM), they are susceptible to damage and even eradication.

At this point we should distinguish between long-term memory and short-term memory. Cognitive psychologists define short-term memory as the first 15-30 seconds. Anything longer is part of our long-term memory. Our short-term memories are important for our day-to-day functioning. To make it to the end of this sentence, you need short-term working memory. But most of what we think of when enhancing memory has to do with long-term memory.

Have you ever lost your keys or phone? All of us have experienced situations where we forgot our keys, our phone, or even where we parked the car in the mall parking lot. The reason we are prone to forgetting these things, is not because we have damage to our brains, or are in the early stages of Alzheimer's, but because your brain was in 'wet paint' mode when you dropped those keys, misplaced your phone, or parked your car. The brain deemed it unimportant almost the instant the event took place. It is only later you kick yourself, and your brain, for not committing that information to memory.

Neuroscience is making incredible progress into understanding better how we create and recall memories, and this is one area of research with the potential to bring about significant improvements in learning and productivity.

The first thing neuroscience has shown us is your memory is subjective and malleable. Many believe memory works like a computer. You experience something, and that event is stored in the brain, ready to be recalled in the future. We like to believe it is as simple as accessing a file on a hard drive, but this comparison is not accurate.

One challenge in artificial intelligence (AI) is having a computer act like a human. The difference between a computer and a human is the ability to comprehend. A computer retrieves stored information, data, pictures, sounds, videos, etc. and retrieves them when asked to find something that matches what it has stored. But the human mind wants to do more than retrieve, it wants to comprehend.

One problem with education is that most courses are geared to the memorization of details, and your brain is not optimized for this function.

Remembering something involves replicating the pattern of neural activity that occurred when the memory was first created. It is not as simple as opening a file drawer and pulling a file out. You must recreate the process and follow the pathway that created the memory in the first place, and the less 'worn-in' those details, the more difficult it is to recreate. Think of a path through the forest. The well-worn path is easier to follow than one seldom used. The brain works similarly. The more well-used the paths, the better you can follow them.

Neuroscientists used to refer to a single memory – an engram – as a physical change in brain tissue associated with a specific recollection. But recent brain scans have revealed it is more complicated. An engram isn't isolated to a single region but is expressed by a colorful scattering across the neural tissue. As Steve Ramirez of Boston University explains, "A memory looks more like a web in the brain than a single spot." The reason for this web-like distribution is because our memories include all the visual, auditory, and tactile inputs which make an experience 'memorable,' and therefore the brain cells encoded are distributed across many regions. (Gibbens 2018)

A useful analogy for retrieving a memory is a jigsaw puzzle. Like a jigsaw puzzle, a memory is waiting to be put together. There are several pieces scattered about that require you to work out how they all fit together to make up a single idea you can comprehend.

I am sure you have encountered meeting someone you met before and remembering their face, but not their name. This is because we have encoded the visual information into our brains but have failed to connect it well to the auditory information. The puzzle remains half complete. It can be something else will trigger the connection of the name to the face, and it only takes you longer to make the association before you find how the puzzle piece fits.

Three paths to better memory retention

As neuroscientist Gretchen Schmelzer explains, for events to make a lasting change, information must move from short-term memory to long-term memory. There are three ways to accomplish this: urgency, repetition, and association (Schmelzer 2015).

Urgency – or trauma, in the extreme – is one pathway to committing memories. When we encounter a stressful event, our body releases a flood of chemicals that creates and strengthens the connection between neurons and synapses helping to embed the memory. It is possible to commit anything to memory this way, even after a single exposure, and remember it for a lifetime. But it is important to understand when a memory is encoded this way, it is connected with emotion rather than a narrative, and this emotional connection can impact how we recall this memory (Schmelzer 2015).

When people say being forced to talk about a traumatic event is like re-experiencing it, they are actually experiencing it again. Our brains can reproduce the chemicals that form emotions which make us feel bad just by thinking of a traumatic event. I call it God's cruel trick because it does not work to the same degree for good feelings. It is also cruel because we can share those negative feelings with others through a story and their brains will also release chemicals producing the same bad feelings.

Think of a bad experience with a boss or colleague at work, someone you feel wronged you. As you now think about this person, and the event which caused the bad feelings, you will experience changes in your body as cortisol, the stress chemical, is released into your brain.

If you now tell this story of how you were "wronged" by this person to your spouse, friend, or colleague, they will also experience the same emotions you had.

This ability developed as a survival mechanism allowing the group to effectively communicate information important to survival. Our ancestors sat around the cave sharing their near-death experiences and how you should avoid this place, that food, or those people.

For example, they might tell of a fierce river current near the fishing spot, which pulled them under, taking their breath away. Only a last-moment grab of a tree branch saved them from drowning. Told to the group, it would bring up the emotions of fear and desperation and those emotions would help to commit the experience also to our memories. By being able to recreate the emotions in other's brains by telling a story was immeasurably important for promoting the survival of our species.

If we consider the power of this ability in the context of the modern world, we see problems. The bad experience with your boss told over and over to your teammates can have a domino effect, turning the entire team negative and resulting in a dysfunctional team. The saying "I can't like everyone or expect everyone to like me" should be banished from your thinking. The one person you do not get along with and who doesn't like you, is the one who will convince the others to dislike you through the effective transfer of emotional experience.

Repetition is also one way to commit new experiences and information to long-term memory. Like urgency, repetition creates stronger synaptic connections and is one of the key ways in which humans learn. Think about all the things you have learned by repetition, everything from tying your shoes, multiplication tables, playing an instrument, driving a car, and becoming proficient at a sport. Everything is accomplished by repetition and the strengthening of synaptic connections.

New research is showing the most beneficial way to learn is using repetition to space it. Cramming for an exam in an all-nighter is unlikely to bring about a high level of retention. What is more effective is reducing the amount we try to commit to memory to smaller chunks and spacing the learning of those chunks over time.

We know the brain prioritizes information. It stores what it believes to be necessary for our survival and well-being and prunes everything else. By spacing learning out over time, you have a greater possibility to move information into long-term memory. Even if the information is first pruned by your brain, revisiting it again will re-create the neural pathways to it. Doing this again and again, over a longer period, will help you retain better the information you are trying to learn.

If you want to optimize the information you learn in a single chunk, you can consider the work of psychologist George A. Miller of Princeton. His paper, *The Magical Number Seven, Plus or Minus Two: Some Limits on Our Capacity for Processing Information* (Miller 1955), is one of the most highly cited papers in psychology.

Miller's work involved experiments that tested the working memory of participants. Working memory is the memory we hold in the brain for processing. It allows you to temporarily manipulate and store information during tasks that require the use of our S2 brain. It differs from your short-term memory because it doesn't just store information – it also processes it.

What Miller concluded from his research was humans can hold around 7 pieces of information in working memory at any one time, plus or minus 2 pieces (Miller 1955). This is known as Miller's law.

Ever wonder why it is much easier to remember a phone number broken into chunks, or your social security number? For example, if someone tells you their phone number as 5026678562 or as 502 667 8562 which one is easier to remember? The number is broken up in chunks. If you are looking to optimize the amount of information you need to remember, you can consider breaking it into groups of between 5 and 9.

But remember it is also important to think about how to categorize the groups of information.

If I ask you to remember what I want on a pizza I ask you to get for me and I say I want tomatoes, deep dish, olives, sausage, peppers, ham, pineapple, and extra cheese, it is difficult to remember. But if I categorize it, like it is on the restaurant menu, it is much easier:

Crust: deep dish

Meat: sausage and ham

Toppings: tomatoes, olives, peppers and pineapple

Extras: cheese

German Psychologist Hermann Ebbinghaus, back in 1885, did pioneering work into memory and is known for his discovery of the forgetting curve, which is a measure of how fast the brain forgets. He found forgetting was exponential over time with the first 20 minutes to one hour resulting in the greatest loss of memory (Ebbinghaus 2013).

Ebbinghaus' research is a stark reminder our brains are not wired to remember anything not directly connected with our immediate survival.

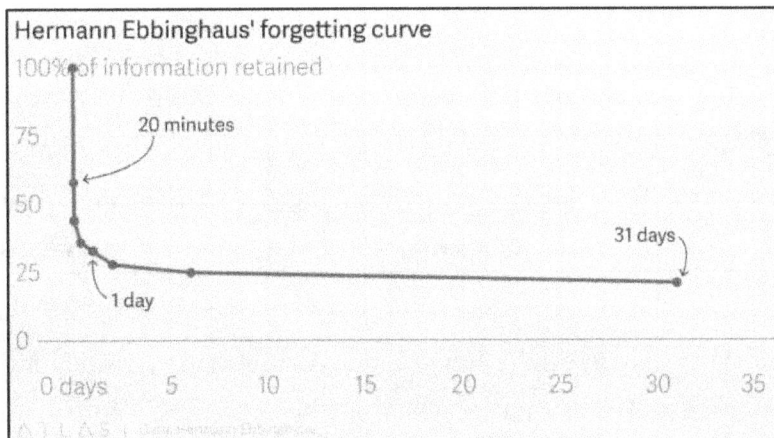

Hermann Ebbinghaus' forgetting curve

He went on to study what could be done to increase our memory retention and found spaced repetition had a significant impact on retention.

Spaced repetition involves splitting information into chunks and repeating those chunks multiple times, with time passing between each repetition (Ebbinghaus 2013).

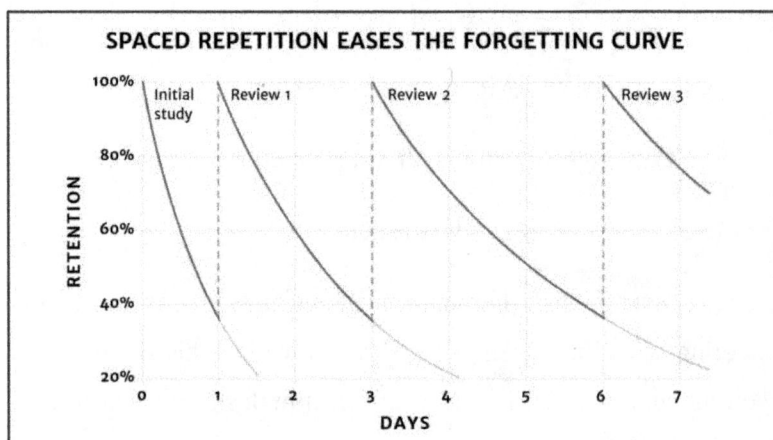

You might think, this is all great, but hasn't anyone improved on this in the 130 years since Ebbinghaus did his research? Thankfully neuroscience has also confirmed spaced repetition of information aids in long-term memory. A 2013 study published in *Frontiers of Human Neuroscience*, found using a timed pattern of three repeated stimuli separated by 10-minute spaces led to what the researchers described as "very rapid LTM [long term memory encoding]" (Kelley and Whatson 2013).

What makes this research so compelling is the way they carried it out. Researchers used a group of students in a biology course and used only spaced learning. They engaged students in a pattern of compressed instructions, with 10-minute distractor activities in-between.

Teachers were instructed to develop learning modules lasting 20 minutes with 10 minutes of distraction in-between for 60 minutes of instruction and 30 minutes of distraction (20 – 10 – 20 – 10 – 20 – 10). Content was repeated in each of the 20-minute speed learning sessions, with only slight variations. Distractions could be anything, but most were physical activities (basketball, juggling, modeling with clay, aerobics).

The results were strikingly good. The students in the one-hour rapid spaced learning group produced better test score results on a standard multiple-choice test than control groups who received four months of traditional teaching. You read correctly: one hour of rapid spaced learning produced significantly better results than four months of traditional teaching, equivalent to 23 hours of instruction. (Kelley and Whatson 2013).

Students raved about the experience. For example, one student explained:

"The lessons are very compressed. For example, the review of my whole biology unit was completed in about 12 min. The nervous system, diet deficiencies, hormones and the menstrual cycle, drugs, and defense from pathogens all whiz by on slides shown at the dizzying rate of 7–8 per min. During the 10-min breaks we get physical, rather than mental, activities like basketball dribbling and teamwork games. So what happens inside your head during Spaced Learning that is different from what happens during a traditional lesson or review session? I can only answer for myself. I love rock climbing. You always have to be aware of what comes next, but you can't consciously think about it. For me, Spaced Learning is a bit like my climbing. I don't try to learn; I don't write anything down, and I don't review. It just seems as if I am seeing a movie in my mind that I have already seen before, and my understanding of the information presented becomes more precise–clearer–when I see it again. In the end, I am left with a movie in my head of the lesson, just like my memory of a climb." (Kelley and Whatson 2013)

Another student commented:

"My first experience of Spaced Learning came in March 2007 when my class re-took our science exams from November 2006. We only had a one hour Spaced Learning review session (which had four months of work condensed into it from the summer before). Most of us did better on the exams after an hour of Spaced Learning review, even though we did no studying at all. I went from an A, B and C to straight A's and an A+. It was amazing." (Kelley and Whatson 2013)

Spaced learning works because it forces you to practice retrieval. According to researchers Diane F. Halpern and Milton D. Hakel the single more important variable in promoting long-term retention and transfer is 'practice at retrieval.' ... Simply stated, information that is frequently retrieved becomes more retrievable." (Diane F. Halpern 2002)

In business, repetition is often overlooked and underutilized. We like to think telling people one time is enough and think it is annoying to others if we repeat ourselves. The truth is one time is never enough.

The first time someone hears something they remember. But it is only for those few moments they hold information in working memory, then the forgetting curve kicks in and it is gone. When reading this paragraph, many of you are thinking to yourselves; "wow, this is a good thing to remember." But let it sit for 30 minutes and most of you will struggle to remember what this great idea you read and promised yourself you would remember was. It is not because you determined it to not be good, it is because your brain prioritized other things, like getting home from work, or cooking dinner.

The same is true with all those important messages needed for people in our organizations to remember. The new strategy, values, mission statement, customer focus, diversity statement, and all the countless other messages everyone should know. How many people in your organization can tell you the mission statement, your values, or your top priorities? An interesting study by London Business School and MIT Sloan, surveying 11 000 senior managers, found that only about 33% could name their companies' top three goals. (Sull, Homkes and Sull 2015)

Remember, the brain is not built to remember, but to comprehend. If you want better recall of what should be important to people at work, you need to repeat until you are blue in the face. Find ways to say the same thing in another way. Put your values and mission into a story people can relate to. Be creative and push the message everywhere and at every opportunity. Never ever think you are repeating yourself. They need repetition.

Association is another technique we can use to encode information to our memory. Associative memory is the ability to learn and remember the relationship between unrelated items. A good example is our association of color with actions, green means go, yellow caution, and red stop. To have this association required the establishment of connections between neurons that represent those associated objects. Once you have been trained red means stop in a traffic situation, the neural links are strong and long-lasting. It has been committed to your long-term memory.

Tomas D. Albright from the Salk Institute explains:

"We are constantly faced with a complex and ever-changing environment. The ability to use information based on learned relations between objects helps us to make sense out of what we see faster and more efficiently. This ability allows us to make the right decisions in a timely manner: Even when presented with a complex visual scene during rush hour we stop at the red light and avoid getting hit by the oncoming traffic." (Salk Institute 2007)

Every piece of information we have in your memory has associations. If I say "Phone" it might bring up the following list of associations:

PHONE: mobile, iPhone, Apple, Steve Jobs, Computer, MAC, Pixar, Finding Nemo

The list likely goes on for some time because we have many associations with those objects are a part of our daily lives. Our memories rely on these associations to aid us in remembering information important to us. If there is no obvious association, then it becomes difficult for us to remember.

A common association aid in school is you use rhymes and acronyms to help us remember. For example, as a new guitar player I had to remember the names of the strings. There are several mnemonic associations for the strings on a guitar, EADGBE. For example:

1. Eddie Ate Dynamite Good Bye Eddie
2. Every Adult Dog Growls Barks Eats
3. Every Acid Dealer Gets Busted Eventually
4. Eat All Dead Gophers Before Easter
5. Eat All Day Get Big Easy
6. Elephants And Donkeys Grow Big Ears
7. Every Apple Does Go Bad Eventually
8. Even Average Dogs Get Bones Eventually
9. Eat a Darn Good Breakfast Early
10. Eat a Darn Good Breakfast Every Day
11. Every Apple Does Get Bitten Eventually
12. Eat A Dog, Get Big Ears

(TheFreeDictionary.com 2018)

These sentences accomplish the same thing, the first letter of each word gives you the string of the guitar. But not every sentence is easy for you to remember. To be easily remembered, your brain must make an association to the words in that sentence. "Eat a dog, get big ears" forms no association to someone who is a cat lover, while "Every Acid Dealer Gets Busted Eventually" likely doesn't appeal to your grandparents. The association must speak to your brain to make it relevant and useful as a memory aid.

New information you are presented with at work, in school, in a sales presentation, your brain struggles to find the association. Often those imparting the information fail to understand we need help in making the associations to improve our ability to recall.

Think of how much more we can accomplish if we can more easily remember information, or present information in a manner which results in a higher level of retention.

Your brain seeks to habituate

There is no such thing as voluntary attention sustained for more than a few seconds at a time.

Psychologist William James

Many of us are subjected regularly to presentations we politely watch and then impolitely forget.

Company updates, new product launches, sales presentations, lectures, and others. Not that we are uninterested in what is being presented. Most of the time we are interested. However, the presenter fails to use urgency, repetition or association to help commit to memory what they present.

Instead we face a sea of uniformly formatted PowerPoint slides, the official marketing-approved, company template: uniform colors, a pre-selected font, company-approved images, and the logo on every page. The purpose of these templates is to make us look "professional." But in the process, we promote habituation which encourages forgetting rather than remembering.

Habituation is a decrease in response because of repeated exposure. The most well-known types of habituation are the tolerance people build up to habit-forming drugs, like heroin and cocaine. The more you ingest the drug, the more you need to produce the same high. But this also happens in other aspects of our lives.

For example, the neighbor's car alarm "accidentally" goes off. The first time you hear it you stand up, take notice, even run outside and look at what is going on. But if it is a regular occurrence, and it proves to be a common malfunction, it will be habituated, and you may not take notice at all.

Habituation takes things out of your conscious awareness and moves them to the unconscious and automatic. It developed as a mechanism for limiting the focus of your brain and preserving energy. The more automatic, the less energy needed.

If something grabbed the attention of our prehistoric ancestors was not efound to warrant constant brain focused attention, it was habituated. The more time you have to get familiar with something, the more opportunity your brain takes to try to move it to an S1 automated process.

The movie industry has fought against habituation for decades by changing the formula for a movie to keep you from getting too used to something and walking out. In a 2010 study conducted by Cornell University and the University of California, Berkeley, researchers found the average shot length (the number of frames running uninterrupted) declined from an average of 12 seconds in 1930 to less than 2.5 seconds today. Not only is the shot length shrunk but the amount of action packed into each of those 2.5 seconds has also increased. (Cutting, DeLong and Nothelfer 2010)

We all have a natural tendency to move in and out of attention and no matter how hard you try to keep your attention to an important company update, you will fail. The movies have it right, to keep attention is hard work and requires a plan to re-orient the viewer's attention. Presentations need to incorporate often "cuts," or changes to keep focus.

Changes in the slide layout, the colors, the fonts, the photos, your own tone of voice and physical movements, are all techniques you can use to refocus your listeners and keep their attention.

The guideline is to adapt the movie shot formula and change something every 2.5 seconds. It does not mean you need to have a car crash in the middle of your cloud computing sales presentation, but you need to change something. If your listeners are multitasking during your presentation, checking their phone or laptop, you know it is time for a "cut scene."

The habituation proof presentation formula

Also consider incorporating rapid and spaced learning as a structure for more memorable presentations. I have coached my clients in sales in a one-hour structure for presentations incorporating spaced learning. Here is the formula I use:

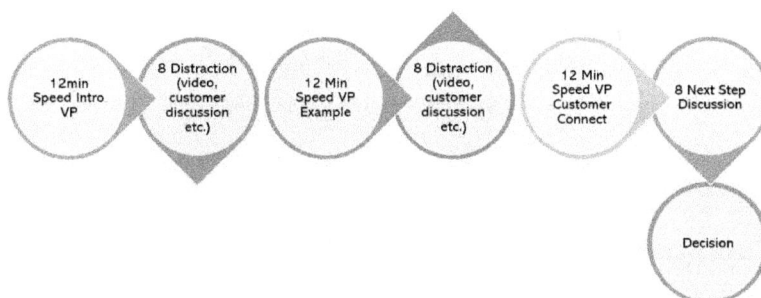

The structure is 12 – 08 – 12 – 08 – 12 – 08 and highlights the value proposition (VP). I repeat it three times, providing "distractions" in-between to allow the listener's brain to absorb content. In each of the 12-minute speed presentations I put 3 to 4 "cuts" to refocus the listener.

By focusing three times on the value proposition, or the main content you want the listener to remember, you are supporting the process of committing the content you want them to remember to long-term memory through spaced repetition.

One challenge of this structure is the discipline and planning it takes. Your brain will fight you as you design your presentation and urge you to go back to the rambling, unfocused, and habitual formula you are used to. It is a challenge to create 3 value propositions conveying the same message but different enough they do not appear to the listener as needless repeating.

It is also important to think of the distractions. Remember in the original spaced learning research they used physical activity as the distraction. You might convince your workmates and colleagues to jump up and throw a basketball around, but your customers are a little bit more difficult to convince. What I suggest for distractions is talking about their business and their priorities. You want something to engage their brains on another level and moves them away from your core message.

This process of rapid content, distraction, and repeat supports how the brain works to commit to memory. By sticking to this process, you will have greater success in getting the listener to retain the content you want them to and if you achieve this, they are more likely to take the action you want them to.

The impact of stress and emotion on memory

Your memory can benefit from low levels of stress, helping to encode memories from emotionally arousing experiences. A study from the University of California published in 2003 found stress enhanced human memory. The researchers showed participants 21 slides from the "International Affective Picture System (IAPS)," a standardized database of pictures used in psychological research to study emotion and attention. They had participants view slides and induced stress using the cold pressor stress (CPS). CPS is a method which plunges the participant's hand into a bowl of ice water for one minute and is a documented low-level method for releasing the stress hormone cortisol in humans. They then tested the number of slides each participant could recall.

The findings revealed those who were administered a CPS after viewing the 21 slides had a significant increase in recall compared to the control group. On average the stressed group recalled 9.2 slides compared with the non-stressed groups 7.9. A 1.3 slide difference out of 21 might not sound like a big deal, but statistically it is significant and proof stress can help us commit information to memory. (Cahill 2003)

We see how lower levels of stress can enhance our memories if induced at a specific time in the memory commit process. However, other research has shown high-stress can also disrupt memory.

A study conducted by the University of Arizona and published in 2006 found stress positively impacted memory for emotional aspects of an event but was a disruptor for non-emotional attributes of the same event. (Payne, Jackson, et al. 2006)

Researchers concluded stress for an emotional experience will help to strengthen or preserve memory, but it negatively impacts the recall of the "neutral" elements of the emotional experience, or those elements are determined by the brain to be incidental. (Payne, Jackson, et al. 2006)

The reason strong emotion helps us to encode memory is because the S1's amygdala (the emotion-processing area of our brain) is more active in emotional situations. Emotion then boosts memory by focusing our attention and perception, which releases the stress hormone (cortisol) and aids the encoding.

It is common for people with traumatic experiences to recall with vivid memory the emotionally charged details of an event, but to report gaps in their memory around details don't have a heavy emotional connection. Memories formed under conditions of high-stress are not the same as those formed under ordinary emotional circumstances. (Payne, Jackson, et al. 2006)

In the experiential role-plays I designed for participants there was always an emotional component. The person they met was angry, depressed, distraught, or indifferent. Not only did this increase the realism of the role-plays but it created an emotional experience which aided the encoding of experience to memory.

There was also a clear element of stress in the role-plays. I asked people to undertake difficult situations and I was there to make it challenging. After several years of practice, I was good at being a difficult employee, twisting words and putting people into the "hot seat" to disrupt their S2 brains. This kept them from delivering on their pre-planned course of action by tripping them up. What I was simulating was stress which so often results from unpredictable reactions of people.

People to my programs often remarked they learned a lot from them, much more than other programs, and didn't need big binders of slides to remember what they learned, they embedded it to their long-term memory. I had stumbled on a formula effective for committing experiences to memory and an enjoyable learning experience.

The brain sometimes needs a nudge to get it to activate and stress and emotion can be those nudges. The trick is not to overdo them and destroy the benefits.

Most of the teaching and training we do with people lacks emotion and stress is too often of a level which induces negative consequences. We force people to sit for hours in a classroom watching presentations which are text heavy and contain little to activate the brain, and then expect them to regurgitate information on a multiple-choice test designed to trick us into selecting the wrong answers.

We believe information will somehow "sink" into their brains, but the truth is most of what we experience (or learn) is forgotten and what is remember is too often random. The value-proposition the salesperson is desperate to get across to the client in her presentation, too often fails to connect and what the prospect remembers is something either irrelevant, your factory looks old, or damaging, your products are expensive.

If we want to remember more, and help others to do the same, it is important we activate the S2 brain. We need to get the higher order brain involved in learning by being better at involving more of the brain.

David C Winegar

The myth of learning styles

One of the big myths of learning is humans have different learning modes or styles. For almost 50 years this idea we can fit people into one of 4 different learning styles; visual, auditory, verbal or physical (kinesthetic), has persisted. A 2012 survey of teachers from the UK and the Netherlands found over 93% believed in different learning styles. (Dekker, et al. 2012) Even outside the education profession you will find a high percentage of people will insist they are "visual learners" or they learn best by doing with their hands (kinesthetic learning).

However, neuroscience has debunked this idea. In 2008 an extensive review by cognitive psychologist Dr. Harold Pashler from the University of California, San Diego, found no evidence to support the idea individuals learn more effectively when teaching is tailored to a specific mode. (Pashler, et al. 2008)

The best way to learn is not via a single mode, but by combining visual, verbal, auditory, and physical, where possible. Remember, memories are like a web across the brain. Covering several areas and functions of the brain, and when we activate learning through the stimulation of more of these areas, there is a greater probability for learning to stick.

Can we trust our memories?

Have you ever argued with your spouse about the details of a past event? You were both there, but somehow your memory of it is different. It is a usual occurrence and the reason is because as much as we would like to think we can trust our memories, science shows us we can't.

One of the most famous examples of a false memory is from a renowned developmental psychologist Jean Piaget who had a false memory embedded by his nanny. While he was growing up, his nanny often told him of the story of an attempted abduction when he was 2 years old.

Piaget could recount in vivid detail events of the attempted abduction. But as it turned out, it never happened. When he was in his teens, his nanny confessed to having made the entire story up. Even though Piaget stopped believing in the memory, knowing it was false, he could not purge it from his brain.

"I was sitting in my pram, which my nurse was pushing in the Champs Élysées, when a man tried to kidnap me. I was held in by the strap fastened round me while my nurse bravely tried to stand between me and the thief. She received various scratches, and I can still see vaguely those on her face. Then a crowd gathered, a policeman with a short cloak and a white baton came up and the man took to his heels. I can still see the whole scene and can even place it near the tube station." (Loftus, The Reality of Repressed Memories 1993)

Elizabeth F. Loftus of the University of Washington is an expert in false memories and has documented how exposure to misinformation induces memory distortion. In research involving over 200 experiments and 20 000 individuals, people recalled a barn in a country setting which had no buildings, broken glass and tape recorders from a crime scene were not present, a white instead of a blue car at a crime scene, and Minnie Mouse instead of Mickey Mouse. (Loftus, Creating False Memories - University of Washington 1997)

Loftus explains it is "pretty easy" to distort the details of what people see by using suggestive information. In one experiment she asked 24 individuals ranging in age from 18 to 53 to remember childhood events provided by parents or close family members. Researchers took three actual events from the childhood of each participant and created one false event.

The false event was the same for each and involved being lost at a shopping mall for an extended period until an elderly woman helped to reunite them with their parents. It was described as a traumatic experience for them with lots of crying.

In subsequent follow-up interviews about their memories 7 of 24 participants (29%) claimed to remember either partially or fully the false event of being lost. There were some noticeable differences in how those remembered the false memories described the events (the real memories participants had slightly more details), but from an on-looker it would be difficult to distinguish the accounts of the true vs the false. (Loftus, Creating False Memories - University of Washington 1997)

Neuroscientists at MIT also studied false memories and published their findings in 2013 in *Science*. What they found might in the future corroborate Loftus findings. The MIT researchers were able to implant in mice false memories of a fearful event and trigger them by activation of the hippocampus. (Steve Ramirez1 2013) Although this research has only succeeded in implanting memories in mice, it is proof science is getting closer to confirming false memory implantation in humans is possible.

Let's consider the implications for our legal system. At this point in history, most legal systems in the world rely on eyewitness testimonials for determining guilt or innocence. "If an eyewitness has "seen it with the naked eye," judges, jury members and attendees take the reports of these *percepts* not only as strong evidence but as fact." (Carbon 2014)

You observe what you know and when there is no prior experience you can overlook it or assume it is something else. Your brain is trained to make sense of things you know and those are familiar you recognize in milliseconds. (Carbon 2014) But with those things you don't know your brain prefers to associate it with something already exists, rather than process it as new, even if when it doesn't match.

It is natural for our brains to work in this way and we would struggle to function on a day-to-day basis if it didn't. Your brain's perceptual system responds to stimuli rapidly and you decide based on it as quickly as possible, the speed of decision-making being more important than accuracy to survival.

Often your behavior is correct, and the actions are taken beneficial, however, it is not infallible. When embedded memories of experiences do not match with the stimuli you are receiving, the brain can get things wrong. Being acutely aware of your brain's propensity to force "square pegs into round holes" and assist you in reconsidering situations before you act (more on to do this in subsequent chapters).

Sleep and memory

Sleep has a big impact on your memories and is critical to successful memory creation and recall. Sleep deprivation affects many people. Researchers at Michigan State University conducted a large controlled study of sleep deprivation, releasing their findings in the *Journal of Experimental Psychology: General* in 2018.

What they found was memories are negatively impacted by sleep deprivation. This to most would seem an obvious conclusion, but two things stood out from the study. First the number of people who suffer from severe sleep deprivation was higher than thought, and second, the negative extent of the impact on memory was greater than expected.

Kimberly Fenn, associate professor of psychology and director of the Michigan State University Sleep and Learning Lab found one-quarter of people in critical jobs involved in completing procedurally heavy tasks had fallen asleep on the job. (Michelle E. Stepan 2018)

An example of a procedural error found by Fenn's team resulting from sleep-deprived individuals was the number of sponges left inside surgery patients. Every day on average 11 sponges are left inside patients who have undergone surgery in the United States. In a year this procedural error alone results in over 4 000 sponges left inside patients.

Fenn's team studied over 230 people in her lab to test the effects of sleep deprivation on sequenced-based tasks requiring systematic, step-by-step, completion. All participants were brought into her lab at 10pm and tested in a predefined demanding procedure. Half were sent home to sleep, while the other half stayed at the lab and were kept awake all night. In the morning they retested the group. The result was a startling jump in errors from the sleep-deprived group.

In the first test all participants completed the procedure, but the next day 15% of the sleep-deprived group failed the test, compared to just 1% of those who slept. Not only did 15% fail, a high percentage (that's 35 of 234 people), but the sleep-deprived also showed a progression in the number of errors produced, something not observed in those who slept. The difficulty the sleep-deprived had in remembering where they were in the sequence when interrupted or faced with a distraction was alarming. (Michelle E. Stepan 2018)

The University of Pennsylvania School of Medicine found one in 4 Americans developed acute, or temporary, insomnia each year. Acute insomnia is difficulty falling asleep or staying asleep for as little as three nights per week for at least two consecutive weeks up to three months. "Whether caused by stress, illness, medications, or other factors, poor sleep is common," said senior author Michael Perlis (University of Pennsylvania School of Medicine 2018)

If we take the fact sleep-deprived people struggle to perform cognitively demanding tasks together with the number of people who suffer from sleep deprivation, we get an alarming picture. The next time you go to the doctor, or your car to be repaired, the first question should be, "How did you sleep last night?"

We also need to be honest with ourselves and those in our lives to be on the lookout for the signs of sleep deprivation and seek or offer help. Signs include irritability, moodiness, fatigue, forgetfulness, and inability to concentrate. You might also experience a forced brain shut down for a few seconds, known as a micro-sleep, where you become unconscious for between .05 and 15 seconds without knowing it (Poudel, et al. 2014). The implications of micro-sleep are potentially catastrophic.

If you notice these signs it is important to recognize the risk posed from a lack of sleep and if injury or safety is at risk, remove yourselves and others from the task.

Most people can recover from mild insomnia with no medical intervention, but if it becomes chronic, occurring over three nights a week for three months or more, then medical advice should be sought. There are many treatments for sleep deprivation these days, ranging from medication, to apps and even brain-wave stimulation devices.

Sleep is also important for consolidating memories. It is known your experiences are replayed in your sleep much like the replay of a movie. This replay in your dreams helps to strengthen the connections between brain cells.

Research conducted in rats have observed neuron firing patterns in the hippocampus are reactivated in sleep. This reactivation acts to induce synaptic plasticity and promote the consolidation of recently encoded information to the memory. During sleep, the rats were replaying maze patterns they were learning to navigate, helping to commit the path to memory. (Sadowski, Jones and Mellor 2016)

Sleep also allows the brain time to filter and prioritize memories. A lot of what your brain does while you are sleeping is also forgetting, sifting through unneeded or unimportant connections. You need sleep to clean up your brain and prune away the connections no longer deemed necessary (such as where you put your wallet yesterday) so there is room for more learning the next day. (Luisa de Vivo 2017)

Babies and children sleep much more than adults because everything is new to them and they need more time to both consolidate and prune. As your experience grows, you are taking in fewer new things and the time needed to process decreases. Many adults function well on just 5 hours of sleep a night, whereas babies need over 12 hours and young children 10 to 12. If you are involved in learning lots of new things, for example in switching jobs, you will find your brain wanting more sleep.

Gut feelings are real

When we try to understand our behavior and those of others it is essential to keep in mind our S1 brain's desire to be energy prudent. One system you use to be energy efficient is the gut-brain predictive system which allows for a quick decision based on a feeling or intuition.

It is tempting to think of those "gut" feelings as a primitive, magical, or religious-based thinking. But this is a myth of the cognitive process. Emotions are not responses to be ignored or corrected by rational thinking. They are simply appraisals of experiences. "Research suggests the brain is a large predictive machine, constantly comparing incoming sensory information and current experiences against stored knowledge and memories of previous experiences, and predicting what will come next, in what scientists call the 'predictive processing framework'" (Mulukom 2018).

You use your "gut feelings" to help you make quick decisions to save your life or help avoid risk. According to new research out of the University of Florida it is our gut that creates this feeling.

Researcher Linda Rinaman explains, signals transmitted along the gut-brain pathways using the large vagus nerve network are powerful influences on emotions and behavior, particularly in response to worrisome or threatening stimuli and events. The vagus nerve is part of an elaborate protective system that helps shape decisions by prompting us to slow down and re-evaluate a situation or avoid it altogether. (Mulukom 2018)

To understand the gut-brain system in simple terms think about a situation where you are driving in your neighborhood, and you are about to approach a blind corner. This corner is well-known to you and a corner all the neighbors complain is dangerous and just waiting for a serious accident. As you approach the corner today you get a bad feeling in your gut and slow down. Turning into the corner, a large truck backs out of the driveway unaware you are there. You slam on the breaks and swerve just in time to avoid an accident.

You thank the stars you didn't go faster into this corner. If you had been driving faster, you would have plowed head-on into the back of the truck. At this point you think something, or someone was watching over you warning you of imminent danger.

This is an example of the predictive nature of our brains triggered by our gut. The brain matches your current situation to your stored past experiences and your body sends signals that act to predict outcomes. Your brain is your personal crystal ball on the lookout for danger.

Intuition or "gut" feeling improves as you build your internal database of experience. The more experiences you have, the more potential for your gut feelings to be accurate.

Should we then trust our gut feelings and rely on for our decision making? The answer is more complicated than a simple yes or no. Over-analysis can hinder the decision-making process and your own cognitive biases will influence your behavior and result in systematic errors in thinking.

Stereotyping is an excellent example of a cognitive bias and how your brain uses culturally embedded beliefs to misinterpret the signals from our gut.

Stereotyping is defined as a widely held and oversimplified image or idea of what someone or something is like. Stereotypes are reinforced in our brains by the culture we live in and are inescapable. These brain "patterns" are the ones we go to when making snap judgments of others, and they are challenging to overcome. (Amodio 2014) They are a shortcut to evaluating a person or group. We know this "type" of person is this way so there is no need to waste energy in assessing their abilities or worth.

This phenomenon is well known in the world of psychology as the fundamental attribution error, or our tendency to overemphasize personal characteristics and ignore situational factors when judging people's behavior. For example, we see a person giving money to a homeless person on the street; our first reaction might be she is a "helpful and caring person" and a person cuts us off in traffic is a "real jerk." We think people who do something we view as right as a good person and those who do something we view as wrong as bad. We ignore the situational factors at work. The person cutting us off in traffic might be late for an important meeting, or on the way to the emergency room, but our brains do not consider this, preferring to make our snap judgments.

The fundamental attribution error has been around since the 60s in psychological research, but neuroscience has also confirmed this phenomenon. Cognitive researcher Joseph Moran of Harvard published a study in the Journal of Cognitive Neuroscience in 2014 which found we gravitate towards a view of people's behavior as a defining characteristic of their mind and not a product of the situation. The findings matched research previously carried out by psychologists (Moran, Jolly and Mitchell 2014).

Dr. Moran explains:

"This work serves as a reminder to consider alternative explanations for someone else's behavior. Perhaps we can take a deep breath and try to imagine what situational forces caused someone to act like a jerk. After all, if we were in their shoes, we'd probably have a good understanding of why they acted that way. It is easy to see ourselves committing the fundamental attribution error, and others doing so in everyday life, but harder to take the time to take the perspective of others... I think a good take home point is that we might have a cognitive system designed to rapidly, efficiently and automatically understand others' behavior in terms of their intentions, and that this system might lead us astray when those dispositions are in fact absent." (Cognitive Neuroscience Society 2013)

If we are aware of our cognitive biases, we can work to overcome them and use our intuition and gut feelings more wisely. We must also consider our old S1 brains are not always evaluating situations according to a modern world. For example, the chocolate cake on the table. Your S1 brain will tell you to go ahead and eat all of it right now. It is worried you might not get another chance to get all those sugars and fats and so you better act now and eat it. Pre-historic man would have just gorged on it, even to the point of being sick. But today we know better and can make a better assessment of situations and not just give in to our S1 brain's impulses.

Therefore, for every situation, it is essential to consider if your intuition is correctly assessing the situation. If it is evolutionarily old, involves a cognitive bias, and you don't have expertise in it, then it is important to force your brain to move it up to your S2 brain where you can use your analytical abilities to make a better-informed judgment. (Mulukom 2018)

It is also interesting to note research has shown that one reason adolescents are more prone to making poor decisions is that the gut-brain connection is not working the same as it does in adults.

In a study conducted at the Duke Center for Cognitive Neuroscience and published in 2014 found teens have a harder time assessing the trustworthiness of people than adults. The researchers found there was a disconnect in the brain resulting in regions not connecting to deliver an accurate assessment. Although this study looked only at trustworthiness, researchers concluded this was a clear sign that adolescence was a period of reorganization of our neural circuits which underly socioemotional behavior. In other words, teens appear to have a weaker gut-brain connection and this weaker connection may help explain why teens are prone to making riskier social decisions (Kragel, et al. 2015).

The scientific evidence supporting adolescents' decision-making is unique, and a normal part of the maturing of the brain, is growing. In an fMRI study neuroscientist found the overall size and gross organization of the brain to be similar in adolescents and adults. However, in adolescents, dynamic changes in brain structure, function, and features of neural systems are occurring. These changes are known to impact impulse control, working memory, and complex reasoning. As researchers explain:

"Although adolescents appear to have full access to many of the cognitive foundations of decision-making, several aspects of decision-making such as intertemporal choice, prospective evaluation, and integration of positive and negative feedback are not yet tuned to typical adult levels. Still other processes that inform decision-making are uniquely amplified during adolescence: learning from direct experience, reward reactivity, tolerance of ambiguity, and context-dependent orientation toward risk in exciting or peer-laden situations." (Hartley and Somerville 2015)

The consequence is the S2 brain is constrained when undertaking tasks involving heavy deliberation, integration of complex information, and empathy. These limitations can lead to risky behavior and ill-formed choices in adolescents and offer a neuroscience explanation to why teens engage in risky behavior. Their brains made them do it.

YOUR BRAIN AVOIDS THINKING

The more skilled at doing something the less energy your brain expends. Built into our brains is the economy of action. As Daniel Kahneman described it, there is a general "law of least effect" that applies to cognitive and physical exertion. If there are several ways of achieving the same goal, humans will gravitate towards the course of action that requires the least effort. Humans are lazy by design. (Kahneman 2011)

Doing new things always requires the use of energy. It is only through constant attention and practice can we convert an S2 task over to an automated S1 habit. Your brain wishes to convert everything to a habit because once a habit is formed, the cost of doing it drops.

Think about driving a car. Most of you reading this have gone through the life experience of learning to drive. Do you remember your first driving lesson? It was a mentally intensive experience. If, like me, you learned to drive on a manual transmission car with a gear shift and clutch, even more so. Remember how your mind worked feverishly to take in the stimulus surrounding you. Other cars, pedestrians, bicyclist, lights, noise, smells, and the physically demanding side of coordinating your hands and feet. Push the clutch in, select the gear, put your hands on the wheel, look out for other cars, people, dogs, and children. Let the clutch out, slowly and smoothly until it starts to take, press the accelerator to give it a bit of gas so the engine doesn't stall. Watch out for obstacles on the road, notice the truck in the middle of the street, the person opening their door in the parked car in front of you. It all combined to produce a mentally taxing experience for your brain. The first few times you likely found yourself exhausted after a single one-hour session.

Fast forward to today and driving is almost entirely automatic. You can drive to work or your local grocery store on autopilot without thought. You might even get there and wonder, how did I do that? All those previously mentally demanding actions have transferred to your S1 brain becoming automatic and habituated, and more importantly, energy efficient. Think how little you would accomplish each day if required to expend as much energy to get to work that you needed for your first driving lesson? This is why your brain automates and why it is a necessary human process.

You S2 Brain is a limited resource

Your S2 brain is a limited resource. It is impossible to engage your thinking mind and focus for extended periods of time. It is too exhausting, and your S1 brain will fight the use of energy by shutting down blood flow to your S2 cognitive brain as quickly as it can.

The most energy-intensive cognitive task for human beings is self-control. Controlling your thoughts to direct your behavior is difficult and unpleasant. Psychologist Roy Baumeister studied cognitive effort and, in a series of experiments, demonstrated that effort of will, or self-control, is tiring.

If you must force yourself to do something, you are less willing or less able to exert self-control when the next task comes. For example, Baumeister found when subjects were asked to watch an emotionally charged film and told to repress their emotions. This act of repression resulted in poor performance on cognitive tests given afterwards. (M Mauraven 2000)

Physical stamina was also found to be negatively affected by the act of suppression. The ability to endure a physically difficult task was greatly reduced after the mental strain of emotional repression. Baumeister termed this phenomenon 'ego depletion,' explaining the mind has limited resources and when used up self-control is impaired (M Mauraven 2000).

There has been recently some debate about the validity of ego-depletion. A few studies tried to replicate Baumeister's experiments but failed to find any evidence for ego depletion (Friese, et al. 2018). Baumeister argued his original protocol was rejected and if followed would have confirmed his original findings. The debate will continue and take years to settle. It is my belief ego-depletion will be eventually confirmed in Baumeister's favor. One reason I believe it will be confirmed is because of the evolutionary connection.

University of Toronto neuroscientist Michael Inzlicht explains:

"As an organism, we need to meet multiple goals to survive. We're not solely focused on finding food or finding mates, sleeping, or pursuing our passions in life. We need to do all these things to be a healthy, thriving species. Because these multiple goals compete with one another [for our time], we need a mechanism in place that signals, 'Hey, stop doing that thing and do something else.' That mechanism could be fatigue." (Inzlicht 2018)

Fatigue is the brain running out of mental reserve for continuing a task it determines you are spending too much time on at the expense of others necessary for survival. If you are at work over 12 hours you likely feel tired, even if all you are doing is sitting at a computer typing. This is your brain's way of telling you that you need to stop and get something to eat and sleep, two things necessary to be healthy and thrive.

What neuroscience tells us about self-control matches with what Baumeister observed, it is brain-taxing and hard to sustain. In three separate fMRI studies published in 2013 neuroscientists required subjects to engage in a mentally taxing task and then complete a "Stroop task", a standard psychological test to measure reaction time. In all cases, a marked decline in performance on the Stroop task followed mental exertions, confirming the underlying assumptions about ego depletion observed by Baumeister (Elliot T Berkman 2013).

Remembering your brain, and those of others, cannot sustain demanding tasks is important to productivity initiatives. Too often we push ourselves and others from one demanding task to another without allowing adequate time for the brain to recover. Neuroscience studies have shown to function at an optimal level, the brain needs to go into a resting state after demanding tasks (Elliot T Berkman 2013).

Bra*in*sights

Researchers at the University of Southern California found when we are resting our brains are far from idle and unproductive. This downtime is used to make sense of what has been experienced, to surface fundamental unresolved tensions in our lives, and reflect. These moments of introspection give you the ability to solve tough problems (Mary Helen Immordino-Yang 2012).

Have you ever experienced an 'ah-ha' moment while in the shower, or walking the dog? Perhaps it was the Sunday crossword puzzle you were working on, or a work-related problem that perplexed you for days, but in the shower the solution popped into your head without effort. You could experience this breakthrough because your brain was in a resting state of processing and able to make sense of new information.

Downtime for the brain is vital for memory. Dozens of studies (Payne 2011) confirm memory depends on sleep. Perhaps you noticed in school those vocabulary terms you struggled to remember the previous day came easily to mind after a good night's sleep. During sleep, the brain is busy consolidating accumulated data and rehearsing recently learned skills. Committing to memory those experiences determined to be valuable.

Think of the implications for your daily life. How often are we put into demanding tasks and provided little or no time for processing and internalizing what we have experience? It is common for organizations to push people to produce in a limited time frame without allowing time to recover from a task before being put into the next.

For example, in my field of training and development it is not uncommon to send people to training sessions in the morning, fill their heads with new information over hours of cognitively demanding tasks, then send them straight back to work in the afternoon. There is no time for information consolidation with the result being the information is quickly deleted from the brain.

If you want to hack your brain to more efficiently internalize what you learn then allowing your brain to rest between tasks is important. It is what is necessary for the creation of the new neural connections to form the pathways allowing you to use what you have learned (Josef Sadowski 2016).

Research has shown that sleep allows the brain to sift through memories and be selective about what it internalizes and remembers. The brain 'prunes' connections when you sleep, determining in the process what should be kept and what can be deleted in an effort to wipe the slate clean for the next day's experiences. The brain's 'housekeeping' at night is indispensable to achieving higher level of brain function.

Babies and children require more sleep. Children are not sleeping more because they are lazy; it is, in fact, the opposite. They need more sleep than adults because their brains are experiencing and learning more. For children, they are busy creating the database of experiences they will use over their entire lives. So much of what happens in a day is new for them. Processing is mentally demanding and necessitates extra sleep to make sense of and construct experiences for future reference. (Howard P. Roffwarg 1966)

When working with others, also know we are not equal in our ability to recover from demanding tasks. The research done so far in this area reveals there is a 'hangover' effect that can be longer in less cognitively resilient individuals (Thomas P. K. Breckel 2013).

It is natural for some people to recover more quickly than others and recovery for some tasks will take longer than others. Those tasks that are demanding but you have more experience with, you recover faster from. For example, if you're used to driving in heavy traffic every day, you will recover sooner than if it was a new experience. (Thomas P. K. Breckel 2013)

Exploitation vs exploration and its Impact

Neuroscience has also shown why our self-control wanes over time, suggesting the roots are based in evolution. We balance the needs for exploitation with exploration. The brain weighs the cost of doing something with the likelihood of reward. The perceived danger for the brain always is we will spend too much effort on something new (exploration) which fails to produce a reward (exploitation).

Think again about the diet you promised yourself you'd start. You were able for the first few days to stick to it, but then when your brain felt the impact, a lack of calories and energy, it reevaluated if it is worthwhile to continue, and concludes it is not. You run to the fridge and take a big bowl of ice-cream.

So how do you hack your brain to improve on your ability to stick with and accomplish things? What the research tells us is we must transform the way our brain thinks about goals. We need to move from a 'should' goal to a 'want' goal. Want goals are more acceptable and less resisted by the brain because they are perceived as enjoyable and meaningful. But it is difficult to override our brains and even more difficult to override the brains of others.

Ego depletion leads people to 'wants' which are immediately gratifying (for example, watching a movie or eating a chocolate bar) as opposed to 'shoulds' that are not as instantly gratifying but have higher total future benefits – for example, watching a documentary film or eating a salad instead of a burger (Michael Inzlicht 2016).

Without reward to balance the increasing aversiveness of work, people prefer immediate pleasure over long-term potential reward, known as hyperbolic discounting. If I ask you if you would rather have $5.00 now or $10.00 in a week, most of you will choose the $5.00 now (Adrian M. Haith 2012). The 21-year-old you has a hard time imaging the needs of the 65-year-old retired you and you buy those completely unnecessary, and expensive, pair of shoes rather than contributing more to your 401K.

This tendency goes back to our pre-historic past. When we saw an antelope on the plains ready to be taken for food, we didn't leave it to be killed and eaten at some future point in time; we saw, killed, and ate it now. The thinking being who knows if it will be there when I come back. It is better to avoid the risk and use the resource immediately.

In classic economic theory, people discount future reward value exponentially. Your brain is wired for now. Neuroscientists have discovered it lights up like a 4th of July fireworks display when stimulated by the power of getting something now. Scientists agree the brain's aim is to "maximize the expected value of the reward." The way it maximizes value is by getting it sooner rather than later and our brain has a built-in mechanism to push us towards immediate satisfaction. (Adrian M. Haith 2012)

If you want to hack your brain to break out of immediate gratification, you must be convinced of overwhelming future benefits. Waiting it out, or exploring the future, needs to have an excellent possibility to generate rewards worth the risk of waiting.

In a 2010 study of smokers, researchers looked at persons who smoked at least a half of pack of cigarettes a day. They asked them to record each day when and how many cigarettes they smoked. In the next phase, they asked them to suppress all thoughts about smoking. The results were, as could be expected, those who suppressed smoked significantly fewer cigarettes than the control group who were not asked to suppress. In the final phase, the students were no longer required to suppress their thoughts about smoking. The result was a significant increase in the number of cigarettes smoked.

The researchers also measured stress levels. Unsurprisingly, when they were suppressing thoughts, stress levels skyrocketed. The conclusion was that suppression is not a long-term strategy for dealing with unwanted thoughts (Adrian M. Haith 2012).

A better plan to break habits is to replace them. If you have a child who is overeating and needs to lose weight, the key to getting them to stick to a diet is to replace the thoughts of food with thoughts of doing something else which offers another reward. Perhaps you focus them on an activity you know they like. A video game could be a good starting point (although you should be careful not to replace one addiction with another). You could also enroll them in a martial arts program strong in mental discipline. The key is to hack their brains to channel the thoughts you want to change towards something else that will 'distract' their brain. With enough practice, the brain will eventually form a habit replacing the urge to eat – but it takes consistent reinforcement and patience.

Habit is something the brain loves to do because it is energy efficient and not all habits are bad. When we hear the word 'habit' we too often think of bad habits and not the many good ones we have. For the brain it is not thinking about good or bad, it is just thinking how this can be made automatic.

To support the process of replacing a habit, break down the new habit into smaller manageable chunks and celebrate the small steps along the way. For the overeating child, rewarding them for achieving a belt in their karate program is a small reward towards the larger goal of losing weight. The martial arts program my son started at seven understands this well and uses it to keep students motivated until habits are formed. The first three belts for him came quickly and without too much pain. The acquiring of belts kept him motivated in the difficult time before habit was formed. Now he is 16, and only 2 belts away from a black belt. He has been working toward the red belt for two years. It is more difficult to get, but it doesn't matter because the habit of going to his martial arts training three times a week has been established and automated.

It is also about planning. When you create a plan for what to do when you consider engaging in negative behavior, you begin the process of rewiring your brain for a successful change. In this process we switch from a habitual to a goal-directed action. An example is getting home from work every day. It's a habit. You need not think much about it. But sometimes it requires a change, a traffic jam, or a train disruption, and then you switch off 'autopilot' and turn on goal-directed actions.

Regulating one's behavior to effectively direct it towards a more beneficial outcome is something that has been around for a long time and science supports it is possible. It only requires willpower to overcome impulsive reactions to stimuli. Realizing your brain, your S1 lizard brain and its propensity to want to react automatically and emotionally to stimuli, is the first step.

At about age three, children start developing self-regulation, with many parents noticing the level of attention focus. As we mature the amount of self-regulation we have varies from person to person. One of the most famous studies is the delayed gratification study published in 1972 known as the 'marshmallow experiment.'

Preschoolers were offered a choice between one small reward provided immediately or two if they waited 15 minutes, during which time the tester left the room with the marshmallow on a table in front of them. Some children immediately ate the marshmallow when the tester left the room, others would stress over what they should do, showing physical signs of anxiety as they tried to resist temptation. (Mischel, Ebbesen and Zeiss, Cognitive and Attentional Mechanisms in Delay of Gratification. 1972)

The marshmallow experiment is often used as proof those who can resist temptation and instant gratification tend to be more successful in life, and there were some follow-up studies with the original participants reporting this as a finding (Casey, Somerville, et al. 2012). But a replication study published in 2018 in the journal Psychological Science found when you removed the environmental conditions the children grew up in, there were far fewer statistical differences between the success of those who delayed gratification and those who did not (Watts, Duncan and Quan 2018).

What we can learn from the marshmallow experiment is the power of distraction. Psychologist Walter Mischel analyzed the results of the original experiment and concluded in a book published in 2014 (The Marshmallow Test: Mastering Self-Control), the value in the research was not in what people later achieved, but in the process those who delayed gratification used to, as he puts it, 'distract' themselves. "Four-year-olds can be brilliantly imaginative about distracting themselves, turning their toes into piano keyboards, singing little songs, exploring their nasal orifices" (Mischel 2014). This distraction is used to refocus the mind away from an obsession with the 'marshmallow,' what our brain desires, towards something that can act itself as a satisfying distraction.

Using conscious planning, or what Mischel refers to as 'if then' scenarios, has been shown to be useful for goal attainment, even when requiring a forced break of habit (Papies and Aarts 2016). 'If than' scenarios are when you make the conscious decision when you are faced with a habit you what to change to attach a trigger to it. This trigger will force your brain to move the habituated behavior from being automatically processed by your S1 brain, providing instant gratification, to your S2 brain where it can be redirected to a more desirable behavior. The behavior at first will be a form of delayed gratification, but over time, if successful, will also be habituated and automated.

For example, if you want to make taking critical feedback less painful, you could create an 'if then' scenario including breathing and visualization. First you would create the trigger, if you feel upset by critical feedback, you will resist the temptation to respond by taking three deep breaths, closing your eyes, and imagine being at a peaceful mountain overlook. Only after this will you decide if you respond and how you will respond.

Conscious awareness and self-regulation can be achieved also through mindfulness and meditation training which can strengthen the executive (S2) control process required to support goal-directed actions. Recent neuroscience studies support the idea contemplative practice does help to strengthen our executive control.

An fMRI study published in 2012 in Frontiers in Human Neuroscience concluded persons with greater meditation experience had increased functional connectivity in areas responsible for attention. This suggests the brain regions responsible for these functions were developed more highly by persons who actively practiced meditation. The authors of the study concluded "repeated engagement of relevant brain networks over time induces neuroplastic changes that mediate positive cognitive, emotional, and behavioral outcomes" (Hasenkamp and Barsalou 2012).

By planning in advance what you will do when a tempting thought occurs, you can put triggers in place. This will help you shift from habit to goal-directed action.

One technique is to use a physical body trigger. Place a rubber band around your wrist and when you have a thought you want to replace, snap the rubber band immediately. Your changed behavior will kick into action by being associated with the rubber band. Eventually, you will rewire your brain and not have to use the physical reminder and your brain will slowly move away from the thought you wish to suppress.

Labeling Emotions

Self-regulation is also at the foundation of learning to control our emotions.

Talking about emotions has been at the foundation of psychotherapy for centuries, if not longer. Discussing emotions is thought to provide insight and regulate them. Mindfulness approaches, dating back thousands of years, offer similar methods for helping to focus ourselves on our emotions to build heightened awareness. The idea is that when we raise our awareness, we can lessen the impact of negative emotions.

There is now neuroscience-based evidence to support talking about emotions to help regulate them. Researchers at the University of North Carolina conducted a meta-analysis of 386 neuroimaging studies of emotion and found when people label their emotions it helps regulate them. They found using a word such as 'anger,' 'fear,' or 'disgust' prior to viewing a negative image caused the brain to retrieve knowledge about specific emotions and attempt to put those feelings into more specific words. (Jeffrey A. Brooks 2017)

The regions of the brain being stimulated were found to be the same regions known to be involved when people try to deliberately rethink or re-appraise the meaning of an initial emotional response. More surprisingly, the group that did not label their emotions showed signs of higher activity in the amygdala resulting in more intense and impactful experiences. The research points to the conclusion when you label your emotions, you force the emotion to move up the brain's hierarchy and involve your S2 brain. By doing this you create an opportunity to reassess the emotion and minimize the negative impact by having greater control over your actions. (Jeffrey A. Brooks 2017)

Unfortunately, the modern world has not looked kindly on the expression of emotion in our everyday interactions with others. In fact, it has been heavily discouraged. Emotional openness is often viewed as a sign of weakness. We are constantly encouraged to not let our emotions show when we are working and interacting with people.

Many of you have experienced 'blow-ups' from people who kept emotions about a person or situation bottled up for too long. But if we help people to express and label what they are feeling, rather than hold it in, you can help alleviate much of the pain, stress, and damage to the person's well-being.

One method that can be used is acceptance commitment therapy (ACT), first developed by psychologist Steven C. Hayes in the early 80s. The goal of ACT is not to eliminate difficult feelings, but to acknowledge (label) and control your reaction to them. To make a mindful effort to minimize the negative impact by not getting too deeply wrapped up in negative emotional responses.

In my coaching business when I did role-plays with people on emotionally charged cases, I could often see people were visibly upset. In some situations, the emotion was so strong you could almost see the steam coming from their ears. In one case we were role-playing a situation with a marketing manager, Anna (not her real name), who wanted to practice giving feedback to her colleagues about their behavior at a trade fair. Anna explained in a recent event, many of the salespeople were not present at the company booth, but were away enjoying themselves with rounds of golf, or tennis, instead of on the floor talking to customers. She was visibly upset by this and her anger was visible as she role-played her feedback to us. The more Anna tried to control her emotions and not show she was angry, the more it became uncomfortable to the rest of us.

After a couple of minutes of Anna's speech, which consisted of attempting to get us to admit our behavior was wrong. I stopped her and asked the group to tell me what they felt about the situation. All confessed to feeling uncomfortable and could see Anna was angry and was obviously trying to suppress that anger. We talked about how Anna could change the tone of her talk and agreed she should start with saying she is angry and the reason for her anger. In other words, to label the emotion.

We reset the role-play and Anna came in and immediately expressed her anger at the group for their behavior. The result was at first shock, but everyone listened and understood. It felt much more natural and the discussion then went in the positive direction of how to prevent this situation in the future.

This role-play happened years before the research on labeling emotion was published but is a strong indicator of the power of labeling and being 'permitted' to show and express emotion. I always tell leaders people don't want to work for a robot. They want to work for a human being, and human beings have emotions. Vulnerability is one of the traits people look for in trustful relationships. Admitting you have emotions and sharing them with others by labeling them is one step towards better regulation of those emotions.

In the following chapter, we will look at the chemical process involved in changing our brains and the part dopamine and the reward system plays.

Your brain minimizes the cost of acting

In a ground-breaking study conducted by researchers at the University College of London, Center for Information and Neural Networks, researchers looked at how the brain interprets inputs to decide how to act. Previously it was thought that the decision to act was dependent mostly on the probability of reward, however UC London researchers found the physical cost to act can influence our brain's interpretation of what it is seeing.

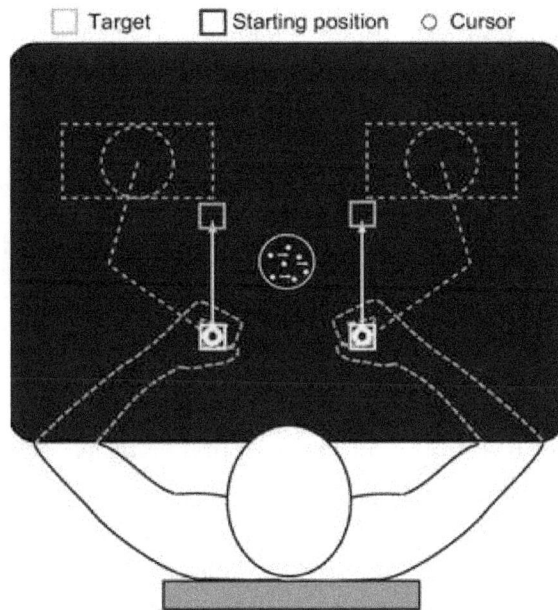

(Hagura, Haggard and Diedrichsen 2017

The experiment took volunteers and asked them to look at computer screens and decide whether dots on the screen were moving to the left or the right. They indicated their choice by moving one of two levers. If they thought the dots were moving to the right, they moved a lever in their right hand. If they thought the dots were moving to the left, they moved a lever in their left hand.

Without the subjects being aware, researchers then slowly added weights to the levers to make one slightly heavier than the other. What happened was the volunteers universally favored the levers easier to pull, so much so it impacted how they saw the dots moving on the screen. The heavier the lever was to pull the less likely the subject saw the dots moving in that direction.

Traditionally, scientists assumed the purpose of the visual system is to take in stimulus to influence your determination of what you see. But these experiments suggest the motor response used to report decisions can also influence the perception of what is seen.

In this case, the effort required to pull the joystick influenced heavily the brain's perception of what it saw. The fact participants were biased by the difficulty in pulling the levers, despite being unaware the levers differed in weight, suggests they were not deliberately choosing the easier option. Instead, the cost to act changed how they perceived the stimuli, and their brains evaluated the cost and gave an 'interpreted view' costing less. (Hagura, Haggard and Diedrichsen 2017)

This research also fits in perfectly with the evolution of our brain and our propensity for laziness. Our brains want to take the low-hanging fruit and expend as little effort as possible, even if it means we are not seeing reality.

The repercussions of these findings for your life is far-reaching. Influencing people's decisions is not simply about promoting the benefits or consequences of their behavior. It is possible to influence how their brain sees the world by making an action more or less effortful.

If you want to stop eating sweets, place the candy jar in a difficult-to-reach place. Research indicates that by doing so you make the candy look less tasty because the brain is telling you it will take too much effort to get it.

Let's also think of the repercussions for the work world. We are all faced with a multitude of tasks every day and can make decisions about how much effort we spend on them. Of course, we have deadlines and bosses looking over our shoulders to see what we are doing. And if you are honest with yourself, a lot of work time is spent in what neuroscientist Robert Cooper explains as the 'blur.' things we do that are not productive. The brain loves the blur because it mistakes mere motion for purposeful work. It confuses the tiresome beehive of activity with making meaningful progress. (R. Cooper 2016)

Email is one of those distractions when we react immediately to it appeases our brain. A 2017 study of 1 500 workers in six organizations by Carlton University in Canada found knowledge workers spend on average 11.7 hours a week processing emails at work and another 5.3 hours at home for a total of 17 hours a week. That equates to over 800 hours a year on email alone. Think now about all those unnecessary hours spent and you start to understand where the day goes and why nothing gets done. (Carleton University 2017)

Immediately reading and responding to our emails is one of those 'blur' tasks. Doing it makes us feel like we are accomplishing something but in reality, it is frequently just a distraction from doing something more productive – something more meaningful with the possibility of a bigger upshot.

I often hear people complain that they don't have any time, how they are constantly busy. The actual statistics show Europeans and Americans are not working more, but considerably less than they did in the 1960s to the 1980s. In fact, every advanced economy in the world is working fewer hours on average. What is happening?

People get caught in the blur of distractions and their brains fooled into believing they are being productive. Their organizations also inadvertently confirm how busy they are and make excuses for their employees which allow them to stay in the blur.

The Global Decline of Annual Work Hours

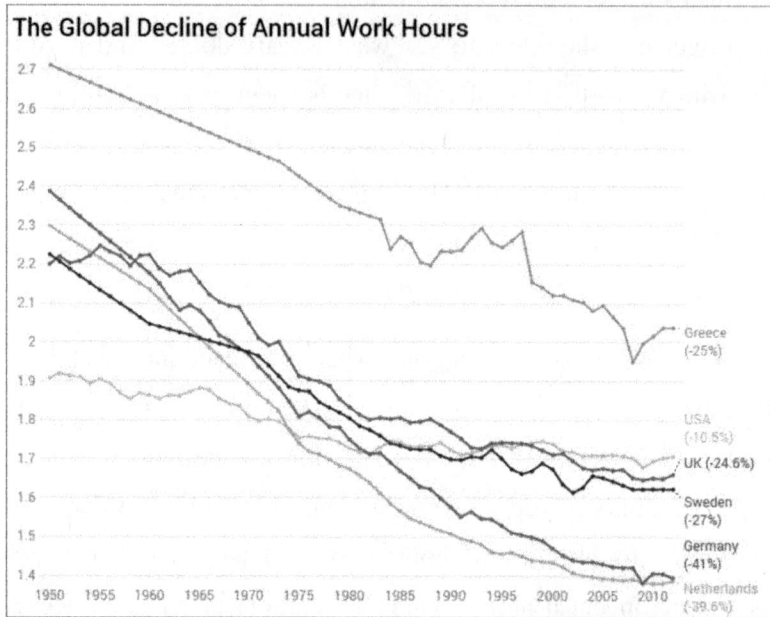

Shockingly, almost half of our time spent awake is occupied with mind wandering. We wrongly think this 'downtime' makes us more creative (Roser 2018)

when the truth is it tends to make us more stressed, and less able to relate to others. Mind wandering may have had an evolutionary advantage of allowing us to better adapt to a changing environment and social circumstances because it allowed us time to mentally contemplate issues remote from the here and now (Fell 2012). However, today most of us have enough free time to not need the constant disruptions we find our minds imposing on us by daydreaming.

In a 2010 study from Harvard, researchers found people were equally happy when daydreaming about something pleasant as when actively engaged in a job task but were less happy when daydreaming about other things (Killingsworth MA n.d.). It was also found even when we are doing a task, we quite often let our minds wander and this deviation from focus unsurprisingly impairs performance as we give in to our inclinations to procrastinate.

To take control of our wondering minds and refocus our attention we must address the emotional problem that is a coping mechanism our brain employees in times of stress. Ever notice how when you are stressed it becomes more difficult to focus? Psychologist Tim Pychyl of Carleton University in Canada and author of *Solving the Procrastination Puzzle*, explains, "We have a brain that is selected for preferring immediate reward. Procrastination is the present-self saying I would rather feel good now. We delay engagement even though it's going to bite us on the butt." (Pychyl 2013)

To break out of the blur of unproductive beehive activity it is essential to remember the weighted joystick experiments and get rid of the easy-to-do but low-value tasks. If we think of our email and social media habits and how most of us have it set to notify us of every new message. The ding and notification message are the low-hanging fruit for our brains. To open those notifications is an easy lever to pull, far easier than putting our brains to work on something much more cognitively demanding.

Taking notifications off automatic is one of the steps you can take to make it much more difficult and less attractive to your brain. We all must check our email several times a day. This is something just part of modern working. But changing it from an auto-check to a manual check will create more effort and help to break the urge to react. It is the equivalent of adding weights to the joystick. Do the same with your phone. Turn email from auto-checking for new messages to manual checking.

It will take some time before you stop looking and listening for the notification and ding, but the result will be a higher awareness of how previously your mind was interrupted and how it caused you to lose focus. You will find your meta-awareness, in general, will increase. Meta-awareness is a term derived from the work of developmental psychologist John Flavell to describe a phenomenon where a person has cognition about cognition or is thinking about thinking. It is an important step in changing behavior as you become more situationally aware. (Flavell 1979)

When you find your mind wandering and are more situationally aware, you can nudge it back on task. What you do when you use these techniques is you change how you engage your brain. You are not structurally altering your brain just yet but are learning how to engage the part better at controlling focus and staying in what is referred to as the 'zone,' a mental state more stable, less error-prone and more productive. (Esterman, Esterman, et al. 2011) (Francesca Fortenbaugh 2018)

Being 'in the zone' is a curious state because, paradoxically, it comes when you are not trying to focus too hard. When you place stress on yourself, or others, to perform, you increase anxiety and it shuts down the receptors in your S2 brain that are responsible for high engagement. Telling yourself to focus harder backfires and makes you less able to concentrate. The potential to work your best is at the point where you are not too anxious and not overly engaged.

The goal should be to optimize your focus when you need to and when it is important. It is not possible for us to be 100% focused 100% of the time – and this should never be a goal. Instead, you should aim to maximize focus when it is important and when it supports better social connection with others. We have allowed distractions into our lives – distractions which divert our focus away from those we should be giving our attention to. In meetings, presentations, and with loved ones, we allow distractions to pull us from the focus and this can be destructive to our relationships and to our performance.

There has been considerable research on multitasking, and it has overwhelmingly found it is not possible. The popular thought is we cannot multitask, we can just do many things at the same time badly, and research supports this. A 2003 study led by Michigan State University found the error rate in a sequence-based procedure on a computer doubled when people were faced with interruptions of just 3 seconds (M. Altmann 2017). Think about how a text message or colleague popping their head into your office, or how a seemingly innocent meeting interruption, affects the quality of work produced.

Gloria Mark of the University of California found a typical office worker gets only 11 minutes between each interruption and it takes on average 25 minutes to return to the original task after an interruption (Mark, Gonzalez and Harris 2005). Next time you are at work, track the number of interruptions you have, and then multiply by 25 minutes – you soon see the day is mostly spent trying to get back your focus.

Multitasking is not even the most accurate term for what we are doing. In most situations what we are doing is rapid toggling between tasks. All this context switching comes at a cost to our brains and performance. Moving from one task to another has been shown to impact people's ability to tune out distractions and impair cognitive ability.

What happens when we engage in rapid task toggling is two things: first we are goal shifting by deciding to do one thing over another, and secondly, we're engaging in role activation or changing from the rules of the previous task to the rules for the new task. Switching between these two functions perhaps take only a 10th of a second but this rapidly adds up in a normal day of work. It may not be a big deal in many situations not requiring a high level of cognitive ability, such as folding laundry or watching television, but when accuracy, productivity, or safety are involved, then it can prove perilous. (Rubinstein, Meyer and Evans 2001)

In 2009 Stanford University research, heavy multitaskers were tested for an ability to sort out relevant information from irrelevant information. It was hypothesized that participants who were used to multitasking would perform better. Surprisingly their performance was found to be worse than those who were not used to multitasking. More worryingly, the heavy multitaskers' brains were less effective and efficient when they were focusing on a single task. (Ophir, Nass and Wagner 2009)

Understanding the negative impact of rapid task toggling (multitasking) from a brain perspective is important in developing good and productive work habits. Interruptions and constant distractions are something important to manage and limited if you are to be highly productive.

It makes sense, but the addictive nature of social media and email is something difficult to break. That 'ding' of a new email or response to one of our social postings is to the human brain, for many, the equivalent of a hit of heroin. We tell ourselves we just need to check. What if it is important? What if someone is waiting for a response from me? It is compelling and at the same time destructive. You can learn to control your brain's addiction to it, like any addiction, but it means putting in place structures and processes to hack your brain into thinking the effort is not worth the reward.

As I am writing this book today Google just announced a new feature in Gmail to address just this problem. The new feature is called "Inbox Pause" and allows you to control incoming email and limit the number of the times it checks for email. More tools for controlling our addiction to task toggling will be rolling out in the months and years to come.

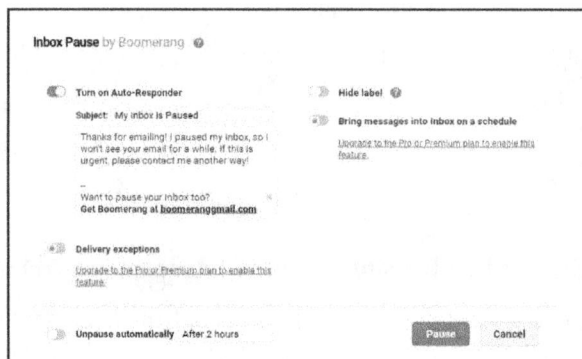

Google's New Mail Pause Feature

David C Winegar

David C Winegar

YOUR BRAIN IS REWARD-DRIVEN

The reward system of the brain is perhaps the most important and insightful area of the brain to study. If you have a good understanding of the reward system you will find answers not only to why you behave as you do, but also what is driving the behavior of others.

The history of the study of the reward system goes back to 1954. Researchers Olds and Milner of McGill University published a seminal paper providing evidence for the existence of the reward center in the human brain.

Their experiment took rats and hard-wired their brains to a device that would deliver an electrical stimulation when they pressed a lever. Researchers believed when a rat received a shock to their brains, it would be unpleasant enough to make them stop pushing the lever. They believed the rat would modify its actions to avoid shock. But what happened was the opposite.

When the rat had its brain wired to a region known as the septal area (a thin sheet of brain tissue in the middle of the brain), they found it repeatedly pressed the lever to receive stimulation. In fact, one rat in their experiment pressed the lever 7 500 times in 12 hours. Some areas of the brain were so sensitive to the stimulation that the rats would choose to receive it over food or sex. (Olds and Milner 1954)

They discovered the neurotransmitter involved to be dopamine. In popular culture, dopamine is the chemical of pleasure, but the current opinion is its role is more complicated than the simple delivery of pleasure. Dopamine is also known to be involved in many of our brain functions including higher-order (S2) thinking, sleeping, mood, attention, and motivation.

Scientists now believe dopamine mediates the motivation towards or away from a behavior rather than the pleasure itself. However, for the simplicity of our discussions, you can think of dopamine as something moving you constantly towards pleasure and away from pain.

The rats pushed the lever to receive an impulse to their brain that felt good. It is the same with many drugs such as cocaine, nicotine, and heroin, which artificially cause spikes in dopamine.

Neuroscientists believe the more dopamine generated by the reward, the more effective it is. The big dopamine release is known as the hedonic impact. Hedonic impact is dictated by two things: the reward itself and by the amount of effort to get it.

Anticipation is a strong reward in itself

Stanford University Robert Sapolsky is a well-known researcher in the study of dopamine. He is most famous for a series of experiments with monkeys showing how anticipation produced a stronger dopamine release than the reward itself.

The monkeys were trained to press a button to receive a food treat when they saw a light. His team measured the amount of dopamine released in a monkey's brain from the moment the light went through to the delivery of the treat.

What was surprising about his findings was the highest levels of dopamine release were not recorded when the monkey received the treat, but when the light first came on signaling them to press the button. The dopamine started as soon as the monkey realized a treat would be coming and ended as soon as they pressed the button. (R. Sapolsky 2017)

Most people believe rewards are the driving force for pleasure, but Sapolsky showed once a reward is expected, for the brain it is less about the reward and more about the anticipation. It is the anticipation which releases dopamine and the pleasure is the anticipation of the reward. The reward itself becomes a mere afterthought so long as the reward is delivered. If no reward comes, then it becomes overwhelmingly important. (R. Sapolsky 2017)

Sapolsky continued his research and wondered what would happen if the reward was not delivered every time but only 50%, 25%, or 75% of the time.

Unbelievably he found dopamine shot through the roof when the monkeys only received the reward 50% of the time. Twice as much dopamine was released in the signaling phase (when anticipating) compared to previously. The 25% and 75% produced more dopamine than when a treat was delivered every time, but less than the 50% delivery rate. (R. Sapolsky 2017)

It all comes down to predictability. How sure can you be you will receive a reward for your efforts? In the 50% scenario uncertainty is high, increasing anticipation. In the 25% of the time delivery you can be relatively sure you won't get a reward, while the 75% delivery will most of the time deliver one.

You may be thinking: I am not a treat-seeking monkey, so what does this have to do with me? Anticipation also is a powerful driver with humans. Let's look at two studies showing how powerful anticipation can be.

First, let's consider online shopping. If listing the disadvantages of shopping online, you would say waiting to get what you ordered is one of the top 3. But this is where the pleasure of anticipation is evident for humans too.

Bra*in*sights

In 2014 interactive marketing firm Razorfish (now a part of Publicis Sapient) released findings of a survey of 1 680 shoppers from the US, UK, Brazil, and China. 76% of people in the US, 72% in the UK, 73% in Brazil, and 82% in China say they are "more excited about online purchases than in-store buys" (Razorfish 2015). The anticipation of getting something in the mail provides more pleasure than getting it instantly in the store. From a pleasure perspective, it's clear why online shopping is so popular.

Las Vegas and other gambling centers all know and take advantage of pleasure of anticipation. Compulsive gamblers will go through withdrawal if they try to quit. Gambling triggers the release of dopamine and gamblers feel euphoric when they are taking big risks and contemplating the reward if successful. It is estimated gambling releases up to 10 times more dopamine than a naturally occurring reward experience. It is the inability to predict reward that is addictive.

There is plenty of evidence gamblers are not successful, and all it takes is a look at the lavish hotels and casinos of Las Vegas to see for yourself they were not built from losing money to you. But casinos excel at convincing you today is your lucky day – all you have to do is make a 'smart' bet. This is where the gambling houses are proficient, even when statistics would confirm your chances of winning are small. A study in 2010 helped to confirm the addiction comes in thinking you can control and beat the system. When you believe there is not enough information to make a 'smart' bet, the dopamine signaling is turned off, the brain finding high uncertainty unpleasurable (Habib and Dixon 2010).

Outside of shopping and gambling, there are a couple of takeaways from this research. First, don't underestimate the power of anticipation. The research is clear anticipation pushes our dopamine buttons and we get pleasure from the idea we might get a reward.

But there is another side to dopamine that is also important to behavior. Dopamine is not only about anticipation but is responsible for goal-directed behavior. If you take the light signal away from the monkey and stimulate his brain to deliver dopamine, the monkey will push the lever. Dopamine regulates motivation, causing individuals to initiate and persevere to obtain something (Salamone JD 2012). Dopamine can be the motivating force which directs your behavior towards a goal you want to achieve.

You have in life always two paths, the path of avoiding pain or the path of delaying pleasure for a bigger reward. Your dog won't delay eating to keep his sporty figure, but you might diet to look good in a swimsuit. What is unique about humans is dopamine generated goal-directed behavior prolongs gratification. Delayed gratification is unique to us in the animal world. As a species we take this to an extreme. Even most of the major religions ask us to delay gratification until after death.

An interesting idea of how you might use delayed gratification to motivate people comes from the University of Oxford. Researchers found the better you can imagine future rewards the more likely you are to choose delayed gratification. The more detail you can conjure in your mind about your expected rewards, the more committed your brain will be to deliver the dopamine to keep you on track. (Lebreton, et al. 2013)

If you want the people you work with and lead to be motivated to achieve their goals, the more detail you can provide about the reward the better. The mistake many leaders make is not reinforcing and reminding people of the reward. One time is not enough. Constant and systematic reinforcement is necessary to keep the reward system primed and working optimally.

The role of reward in learning

Reward and reinforcement both help humans to focus and learn. When we do something pleasurable, the brain wants to repeat this. When we eat a delicious piece of chocolate cake, we want another piece. It tasted good, gave us pleasure, and we want to repeat the feeling. Dopamine helps us to remember how we obtained that pleasure.

For years researchers considered dopamine as primarily affecting immediate mood and behavior, but it in a study conducted at the University of Michigan, researchers found dopamine continuously signals how worthwhile the current situation is and how likely it will return a reward. This information helps people to decide how much effort to put into whatever they are doing (Arif A Hamid 2015). According to researchers, abrupt dopamine increases occur when you perceive stimuli that predict rewards and is a dominant mechanism of reward learning within the brain—a concept not unlike Russian physiologist Ivan Pavlov's dog hearing the bell and salivating at a response to stimuli. "This is basically how we stamp in memories of what the smell of cookies or the McDonald's sign means: predictors of delicious, calorie-rich rewards" (Arif A Hamid 2015).

If we think about it, all your behavior is driven by the reward system. Dopamine is always in the background like a coach sending us the signal of 'good job' or 'bad job' to drive your behavior towards a goal. It is so powerful that researchers at the University of Michigan found rats with almost no dopamine were unmotivated to retrieve food just inches away, even when they were starving. (Arif A Hamid 2015)

Think about the implications for your own motivation and the motivation of others. Why is it sometimes impossible to get motivated to do something we know would be good for us? Even when we know something will help us, we might feel like we simply can't get moving and do it. Think about working with your team and trying to undertake a new initiative you know doesn't have strong support. It is not just the brain's lack of being able to process the logic it is also the lack of dopamine. Our brains aren't receiving a signal that this activity will result in a reward. No neurotransmitting chemical results in no motivation to act.

Intrinsic and Extrinsic Reward

The brain's pleasure area is also wired to two types of stimuli for reward: intrinsic and extrinsic.

Intrinsic motivation refers to the spontaneous tendency "to seek out novelty and challenges, to extend and exercise one's capacity, to explore, and to learn." When intrinsically motivated, people engage in an activity because they find it interesting and inherently satisfying. By contrast, when extrinsically motivated, people engage in an activity to obtain some instrumentally separable consequence, such as the attainment of a reward, the avoidance of a punishment, or the achievement of some valued outcome. (Domenico and Ryan 2017)

Intrinsic motivation is, of course, preferred as it is the motivation we find in ourselves. But intrinsic motivation is trickier to direct in ourselves and others. If we do not perceive something as inherently interesting and satisfying, it is near to impossible to convince the brain it is.

The way in which our brain interprets stimuli and whether it finds stimuli intrinsic or extrinsic depends very much on our experience. For example, completing the New York Times crossword puzzle might for some be intrinsically motivating. They get a sense of accomplishment and it helps with how they interpret their own level of competence. For others, being asked to complete the same puzzle would feel like a burdensome chore. They might be extrinsically motivated to undertake the crossword puzzle with offers of money or prizes, but overall, they are unlikely to enjoy it as the intrinsically motivated people who do it purely for self-satisfaction.

Intrinsic motivation was evolutionarily necessary for the human species, and without it we would most likely not have survived. If we were only motived by tangible rewards, such as getting food or sex, we would be unlikely to undertake new and novel approaches necessary to cope with an uncertain future. For example, we would not search out alternative food sources, mapping of complex game migrations, or taking interest in skills, rituals, and social rules transmitted by other group members. (Alcaro, Huber and Panksepp 2007)

It has also been theorized that intrinsic motivation assists people in fostering a unique personal identity and convenes a sense of authenticity, meaning, and purpose. It is through this process that we expose ourselves to new ideas and challenges. This exposure prevents us from becoming too ideologically rigid and fosters learning, growth, and meaning in life.

In a study at Vanderbilt University, scientists looked at the differences in dopamine levels between those who were identified as 'go-getters' and those who were 'slackers.' The researchers' brain imaging studies revealed the go-getters had a higher release of dopamine when they worked hard for rewards, while the slackers had high levels only in the area of the brain that plays a part in emotion and risk perception. It is this area where dopamine appears to reduce the desire to work, even when it means less reward. (Treadway, et al. 2012)

Does this mean your brain is predetermined to work hard for reward? Well, not exactly. The evidence to draw this conclusion is not yet there. The studies indicate that there is a preference in humans for either working hard or taking it easy and dopamine has an influence on your preference. However, it is possible to override this inherent tendency.

Yale School of Management, professor Victor Harold Vroom, in 1964 developed the Expectancy Theory. This theory states people will choose how to behave depending on the outcomes they expect from their behavior. Vroom assumes behavior results from conscious choices of alternatives and we set about to maximize pleasure and minimize pain. What we expect (the 'expectancy') is the reward will be commensurate with the effort put forth. For Vroom, this is self-evident for people. You innately believe that the harder you work, the more pleasure you will be rewarded. (Vroom 1983)

Therefore, you are most motivated when you believe there is a high probability of receiving a desired reward when you hit an achievable target. You are least motivated if you don't want the reward or believe your efforts will not result in an appropriate level of recompense.

How then do you effectively motivate yourselves and others? To effectively motivate we must constantly remember why our brains have evolved to seek reward and avoid pain. It is your S1 human brain functions largely responsible for motivation to do something or not. Motivation theory has heavily relied on Maslow's Hierarchy which was published first in 1943. Maslow identified different levels of human needs with an idea that we all share the same requirements. He expressed the levels in a pyramid.

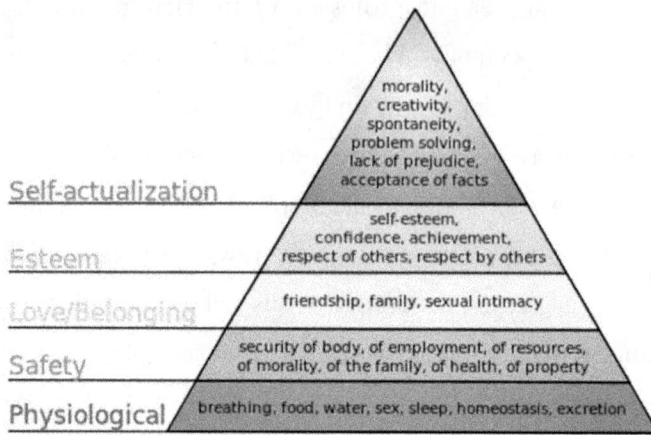

morality,
creativity,
spontaneity,
problem solving,
lack of prejudice,
acceptance of facts

Self-actualization

self-esteem,
confidence, achievement,
respect of others, respect by others

Esteem

Love/Belonging

friendship, family, sexual intimacy

security of body, of employment, of resources,
of morality, of the family, of health, of property

Safety

Physiological

breathing, food, water, sex, sleep, homeostasis, excretion

Maslow's Hierarchy of Needs

At the foundation are basic physiological needs controlled by the S1 brain. As we move up the pyramid, we get to the higher order needs. We are programmed to meet first those at the foundation. Once your needs are satisfied at one level, you seek to satisfy the next levels until you reach the top and self-actualization.

The problem with Maslow's Hierarchy is it is often thought of as a roadmap to human motivation, but research is showing things are more complicated and certainly not linear as Maslow proposed. In several studies, it has been shown for most of us the basic needs are being met and are less of a motivational force than in the past.

In a study involving 238 workers done by Harvard researchers Teresa Amabile and Steven J. Kramer, they found what matters most is not money, safety, security, or pressure to perform, what mattered most was a feeling of making progress, what Amabile and Kramer describe as small wins. (Amabile and Kramer 2011)

In an analysis of the 12 000 diary entries of workers and their description of the best and worst days, the best days all described making progress in the work either individually or as a team. The worst days universally described setbacks. They found on progress days people were intrinsically motivated and on setback days they were not only less intrinsically motivated but also less extrinsically motivated. The setbacks generally made people apathetic and disinclined to work at all. (Amabile and Kramer 2011)

Reward must be greater than pain

The keys to motivation are to ensure the reward is greater than the pain to obtain it. Simple? Yes. But this principle is often difficult to execute in a complicated world. The place to start is to not make a goal too big. Breaking up larger goals into smaller, easily rewarding ones are important. You want yourself, your team, your son, daughter, etc. to experience the feeling of reward from their effort as fast as possible. The faster they get a dopamine infusion into their brain, the sooner they will create the neural pathways to support continuing to make progress towards their goal.

We see this principle at work by many companies in the self-improvement area. Take for example weight-loss companies. Ones such as Jenny Craig promise to help you "lose 16 pounds in just 4 weeks." They do this by breaking down the goal of losing weight into small, obtainable steps that have people seeing the weight come off quickly.

Jenny Craig Ad source: www.jennycraig.com

They provide the food for you, and so long as you only eat what they give you, you will lose weight. It is a simple model limiting your caloric intake which in turn makes you lose weight in small, readily perceivable steps.

Another tactic you can use to increase motivation is to connect the goal to a bigger picture. We are motivated by doing things we find worthwhile and purposeful. The problem is most people take the wrong approach to values-based motivation. They try to impose their values or those of the organization on others instead of making the effort to find out what the values are of the person they wish to motivate.

If you first understand people's values and help them make the connection to their work and the organization, motivation increases. This is what is known as value congruence. In a 2009 study published in the Journal of Applied Psychology, researchers from the University of North Carolina at Chapel Hill found when values are aligned, motivation increases. They also found to influence higher levels of shared values, focusing on the mediators are likely to be more effective than directly trying to convert people to companywide values. Their research showed when trust was present the levels of value congruence were higher. Instead of focusing on trying to convince people your values are ones they should also value, it would be more beneficial to build trust and use it as a mediator for connecting your values to theirs. (Edwards and Cable 2009)

Trust is important to developing a higher level of interaction with others. Focusing on building trust through listening, relating, and genuinely appreciating others will bring better understanding of what their values are. Once you have insight into what values are important, the next step is to connect those to their work to make it more purposeful.

David C Winegar

David C Winegar

YOUR BRAIN IS WIRED FOR SOCIAL CONNECTION

Your brain evolved for social interaction and your behavior is driven by the desire to bond and belong to the group. From an evolutionary standpoint, it makes sense. Humans needed others to survive. The group always has a better chance of survival than an individual. Your brain is wired to look for help and to seek out others who can increase the probability of survival.

One bombshell of neuroscience was an fMRI study published in 2003 in the Journal *Science* (Eisenberger NI 2003) which found social exclusion presented in the brain in similar areas as physical pain. Researchers studied participants playing an online ball-tossing game. The participants were under the false impression there were two to three other real players playing with them but in fact it was a computer that directed the ball tosses.

In the game, exclusion from receiving a ball toss was used to simulated social pain. The game was played while participants were inside an fMRI scanner which was able to identify the brain regions that are activated.

When participants experienced exclusion, or social pain, the area of the brain associated with physical pain became activated. People often describe being left out of a group, or social isolations, as "painful" and what this research suggests is the brain interprets social pain similarly as physical pain (Eisenberger NI 2003).

Researchers at the University of Michigan also found the brain reacts similarly to social pain as to physical pain in the opioid system. The opioid system is the brain's natural pain killing system and kicks in when we are physically harmed. Their research, published in the journal

Molecular Psychiatry, found your painkilling system is also activated when experiencing social pain (Hsu, et al. 2013).

How the Michigan researchers determined the release of opioids in social pain situations was by having participants believe they were taking part in an online dating experiment. Participants viewed hundreds of profiles of people and selected ones they liked. Then they were put into a scanner and told those they liked had no interest in them. Brain scans revealed during those moments, the activation of the opioid system with the greatest release was found in the area associated with physical pain. Another interesting finding was that individuals who had higher levels of resiliency had larger opioid release in the amygdala, the emotional processing area, indicating resilience is a byproduct of opioid release. (Hsu, et al. 2013)

The feelings of pain associated with social exclusion probably evolved in your brain as a mechanism to promote cooperation and appeasement to those who could help you to survive. Engaging in activities that caused you to be socially isolated were manifested in the brain as pain. Your body would respond by transmitting signals that resulted in a feeling similar to physical pain. Just as you try to avoid being hit by another person because it is painful, your brain would avoid behaviors and actions that would cause being rejected by others.

However, social rejection can be completely unwarranted and not always the result of negative behavior. We all know of, or have experienced ourselves, situations of unwarranted social rejection. What many, until now, have not understood is the magnitude of the pain others can inflict on us by excluding and rejecting us. By understanding the chemistry of what is happening in your brain it hopefully provides greater empathy for those who are experiencing social pain. I hope it also encourages you to examine your own behavior and what you can do to help others to avoid the experience of socially inflicted pain.

David C Winegar

In many of my training programs I have run an activity meant to simulate a team under high-stress. The exercise was part of leadership, collaboration, and innovation development programs. Over the years this activity has had participants from more than 70 countries.

The activity placed participants in groups of between five and seven and had them undertake a cognitively challenging task to determine what they were to produce. The task involved decoding four scrambled sentences using a simple decoding device. The stress came in having no idea how the decoding device worked.

The decoder was a cipher called a Caesar cipher, and only required matching up two letters (the code) to replace the letters in sentences. It was an effective coding device in Caesar's time (1st Century BC) because few people could read.

If the team worked together, didn't panic, and used a systematic approach to solve the problem, most could decode in less than an hour. Some even managed to do it in less than 10 minutes. But those teams who let their fear take over and could not control the stress of the situation, often became paralyzed and unable to figure out how to decode the tasks. As they saw other teams completing it, the stress levels increased, and collaboration quickly deteriorated.

During these exercises, I noticed social exclusion played a big role in teams under high stress. When decoding was stressful and time-consuming, people became less concerned with involving people and more concerned with simply getting it done. Part of the exercise was to be creative and I saw many times in teams good, creative, ideas pushed to the side by those more concerned with completing the task. When those creative individuals had their ideas unacknowledged and rejected, I could see them physically shrink away and isolate themselves from the rest of the group. The pain of social rejection evident in their faces and

115

behavior. The result for the team was universally poorer performance in executing the tasks.

Although this was a simulation of a high-stress team environment, I believe you can recognize in your own lifetimes when you have experienced a similar feeling of being rejected by a group. It is important to understand social acceptance is wired to the brain and when we don't get it, it causes us pain. It is also important to understand your own role in helping others to feel accepted, as it can be very beneficial.

I once asked one of my participants from India in a leadership development program how he felt the day of experiential leadership cases went. He replied, "Everything went well until I opened my mouth." This is always something I remind people who I coach to remember. One wrong word, look, or a lack of response can trigger a chain of brain reactions bringing pain. And once you have triggered pain, it is difficult to overcome it.

Our perceived reactions to fear drive interactions

FEAR

Fear is something as fundamental as life itself. Just reading the word 'fear' here probably caused your heart rate to increase and your brain to go on high alert, as it is such a strong emotion for humans. It is a basic emotion that occurs across cultures. It fulfills the function of mobilizing a response to perceived threats. It is important to understand many of our fears are perceived and not realized. To the brain, it doesn't matter. If a stimulus is perceived as a threat, then it signals the brain to act, driving behavior.

In my coaching, I often work with issues related to people's behavior at work. I always start the discussion by asking the person I am coaching what is driving the behavior of the person they have a problem with. Behavior is never random. It is always the result of individual perception of stimuli. Once you figure out what stimuli is triggering the person's brain, you can understand the behavior drivers.

In my experience, nine out of ten times the driving force is fear of something; failure, embarrassment, underperformance, rejection, change, confrontation, and so on. If you understand what someone fears, you can work towards eliminating the fear and the problem.

At the foundation of the fear response are chemicals, with many of those same chemicals also responsible for other positive emotions such as happiness and excitement. This is perhaps why many of us enjoy being scared. Why else would we go to horror movies and put ourselves through what should naturally be something to avoid? What the brain is experiencing in these situations is a heightened state of arousal. This fear feels like the arousal we get from other positive, even addictive, stimuli.

All our responses to stimuli are processed first for the level of threat they pose to us. In fact, most of this determination is done on a subconscious level in our S1 brain. The part of the brain responsible for initiating fear is the amygdala, but it is not the fear factory many people believe it to be. Instead, it is responsible for releasing chemicals that raise the alert to your S2 brain signaling something important is happening and you should take notice. Attention systems in the neocortex (S2) guide a perceptual scan of the environment for an explanation for the aroused state. If your S2 brain's combined processes of attention, perception, memory, and arousal merge in your consciousness and deduce a threat, then you feel fear. (LeDoux 2015)

The brain responds to fear in one of five ways:

1. Avoidance

2. Freeze

3. Flight

4. Fight

5. Appease

The original research into the brain's reaction to fear involved animals where areas of the brain could be isolated and then reactions observed. Snakes and rats who had their amygdala purposely damaged no longer showed a fight or flight response (LeDoux 2015). Interestingly, animals who were administered a shock in a specific environment, such as a red room, showed similar amygdala activation when placed in the same environment but not administered a shock. (LeDoux 2000).

Brain imaging studies of healthy humans with intact brains also found similar findings. When exposed to threats, both actual and perceived, neural activity in the amygdala increased. The body would respond with elevated heart rate, sweating, quickness of breath and other physical manifestations of fear. What was more interesting is scans showed the amygdala (S1) active also in instances where the person was not consciously aware of the fear. As pioneering fear researcher Joseph LeDoux explains:

"In the face of danger, the brain kicks into defense mode, detecting the threat faster than our conscious awareness can ever operate, and sending a host of marching orders throughout the brain and the body, readying all systems to take action." (Schwartz 2015)

According to LeDoux, fear first presents subliminally, where the person is not consciously aware of the threat and has not processed it in their S2, prefrontal cortex. To feel fear, you must be consciously aware of it. Your body may be sensing something is not right, like the rat in the red room, but until the information is moved to your S2 brain and you start to logically process what is going on, it is not yet registered as fear. (Schwartz 2015)

The ability of our brain to sense danger and then signal physical changes to our body is what some would refer to as intuition. Neuroscientist Dr. Joel Pearson of the University of New South Wales conducted experiments by presenting subjects with subliminal emotional information while they made decisions to test our abilities to subconsciously pick up on emotion and use it to guide our decisions.

What Joel's team found was when participants were presented with subconscious subliminal emotional images – that is, images flashed so quickly they could not consciously see them – while they completed a basic decision-making task, they performed better. Not only were they more accurate in the task, but they got better as time went on and gained in confidence. (Lufityanto, Donkin and Pearson 2016)

This research appears to confirm the brain's ability in the subconscious to pick up on emotional signals and assist us in rapidly making decisions and adapting our behavior. The implications for us in the every day are potentially remarkable. Being able to pick up on emotional signals in the subconscious and then modify behavior based on those signals must be considered when interacting with others.

Think about the person in your office you simply cannot get along with. There is just something about them that makes the hair on your neck stand up when you speak with or see them. Whether or not those signals you are getting are based on something real or just imagined, it doesn't matter. Your brain has decided to process the stimuli you get in a negative way and you modify your behavior and interactions accordingly. Now think about the situation from their point of view. What signals are they picking up from you? Likely they are picking up negative indicators and processing you as a threat. You can see how the situation snowballs out of control and a cascade of misinterpretations result in a failed relationship.

I consider our fear response a blessing and a curse. It is there to keep us safe by providing an early warning for what might threaten us. It is also evolved to be overly cautious and default to negative interpretations. There is an evolutionary arms race that is the driver here, and the winner is the one that errs on the side of exaggerated carefulness (Koti 2014). The subconscious warning system is part of our S1 brain and acts as an early warning system. It is possible that our brains are pre-programmed with certain fears or primed to automatically fear certain situations and stimuli.

A good example of how fear negatively impacts organizations is an announcement of downsizing. One of my previous clients, a large electronics manufacturer, responded to poor quarterly results by announcing a cost-saving program with thousands of layoffs. Before this announcement, the CEO had delivered an internal talk to the employees expressing that he wanted to encourage people to take more risks, to raise the level of creativity and innovation necessary for future success. The problem is, the message of risk-taking ran counter to the action of downsizing for the brain.

The brain is wired to not take risks. Risks for your ancestors resulted in injury or death and were to be avoided. The reason it took mankind millions of years to get out of the stone age was due to the unwillingness to take risks. The brain was wired to play it safe. Instead of looking for new opportunities, it tends to stick with what it knows, and thinks is safe.

When a CEO announces that there will be layoffs, it sends people into fear mode with the first reaction being to freeze. Looking around at people listening to the announcement, it is possible to see people with blank stares, deer-caught-in-the-headlights looks. As time goes on, the manifestation of the freeze-fear reaction will cause the opposite behaviors of what the CEO expressed he wanted from his employees.

When you are in fear mode, your brain directs your behavior towards survival and protection. When faced with losing your job along with your basic needs of clothing, shelter and food, your brain directs your actions towards behaviors it believes will minimize the risk of losing those. One of the behavior tools we use is impression management.

How we are viewed by other people has a significant impact on our daily behavior. Impression management is what you do to shape how others see you. It involves creating, maintaining and protecting a desired image of yourself to realize personal gains (Lyle and Smith 2014). It is often a conscious and strategic process carried out to influence the view of others, but it is not only a S2 process. Most times it is an unconscious or habitual S1 process. For example, many people might have a reflexive tendency to complement other people to gain favor (Mark Bolino 2016).

When you face the possibility of losing your job, fear will direct you to undertake actions to minimize standing out as a risk to the organization. One action perceived by many to be risky and avoided is speaking up. Speaking up and expressing honest opinions contrary to accepted group norms often results in negative feedback. People learn to associate speaking up and expressing unpopular opinions with negative outcomes. Silence then becomes a conscious, calculated, and deliberate choice in fear situations (Prouska and Psychogios 2018).

For the organization that is trying to turn around financial performance it is necessary to have more risk-taking. It's important that people feel safe in expressing their ideas, no matter how risky. Most innovations are by default ideas that run counter to the established rules and thinking of an organization. Many even start out as wildly risky ideas. This is known as the 'spark' of innovation. It is through collaboration that the risky 'spark' becomes a viable flame.

When you destroy the safe environment that people need to express their ideas, you destroy the potential for innovation. Without a safe environment people will turn inward and keep their opinions and ideas to themselves. They are more likely to give up and freeze or worse direct their actions towards finding a less uncertain work environment – a new job. The most capable people always have options, and they are the first to abandon a fearful and uncertain environment for something they perceive as less risky to their survival.

Fight-or-flight impacts our health

When we find ourselves in situations of a high threat our bodies go into a hyperactive mode that readies us for the battle. We already spoke about some of the physical manifestations of the fight or flight reactions, but we also need to discuss the impact that those physical changes have on the body, especially long-term.

In the past, when humans were facing down that lion on the savannah of Africa and we had a real chance of being eaten, the brain triggered a series of signals that contribute to emotional processing which sends out a distress signal. This distress signal puts into action body processes that get us ready to defend ourselves against that lion. This S1 triggering happens so quickly that we are mostly not aware of it, the wiring is so efficient in our brains that the brain's visual centers haven't even had a chance to fully process what is happening. Therefore, we can jump out of the way of an oncoming car or move out of the way of a fast flying object before it hits us. We say to ourselves, "I did that without even thinking," which is quite literally correct. (Harvard Health Publishing 2011)

As the initial surge of adrenaline subsides, the second level of defense kicks into action and your HPA axis (hypothalamic pituitary adrenal) shuts down your immune system response. It says, "I don't have time to fight that flu, right now I have to run from a lion." (Anderson 2017)

We don't have to be threatened to be eaten by a predator to trigger the same physiological changes in our body. In the modern world, it is stress from work and our daily lives that is the equivalent of that lion staring us down. If we look at statistics about stress in the workplace, are alarming. The statistical data indicates that stressed employees spend double the amount of money on health care than their less-stressed peers. It completely makes sense given that stressed workers have their immune systems constantly shut down.

It is important to not only manage your own stress levels but also to understand your role in elevating the levels of others. Chronic stress keeps the HPA axis – our central stress response system –active with persistent surges in adrenaline.

The impact on our bodies is increased blood pressure, damaged arteries and blood vessels, all of which increase the risk of heart attack or stroke. When elevated, cortisol – the stress hormone - creates an increase in glucose production and appetite. This is because we need sugars for energy to fight or run from the lion. Long-term, this causes weight gain because we are producing sugar for energy but are just sitting at our desks and not burning it off. (Harvard Health Publishing 2011)

Elevated cortisol levels also reduce the positive brain hormones including serotonin and dopamine, leading to depression and chronic anxiety. When you lose the balance of chemicals in your brain, you lose sleep, appetite, energy, sex drive, and the expression of normal, healthy, emotions.

Understanding stress

Learning to eliminate stimuli that leads to stress is one thing we can do to live a better life. It is not possible to eliminate all stressors. You can't just get rid of a demanding boss, quit your job, stop worrying about money, or loved ones in trouble. But by understanding better what stress is, and what you can expect as a natural reaction to it, you can learn to control it.

Stress is a natural part of life itself. When a stressful event occurs, our bodies start a cascade of biological actions to deal with it. There are two categories of stressors: physiological and psychological.

Physiological stressors are ones that put a physical burden on our bodies. Our heart rate goes up, our breathing gets heavy, we feel cold or hot, and we have pain or other physical responses.

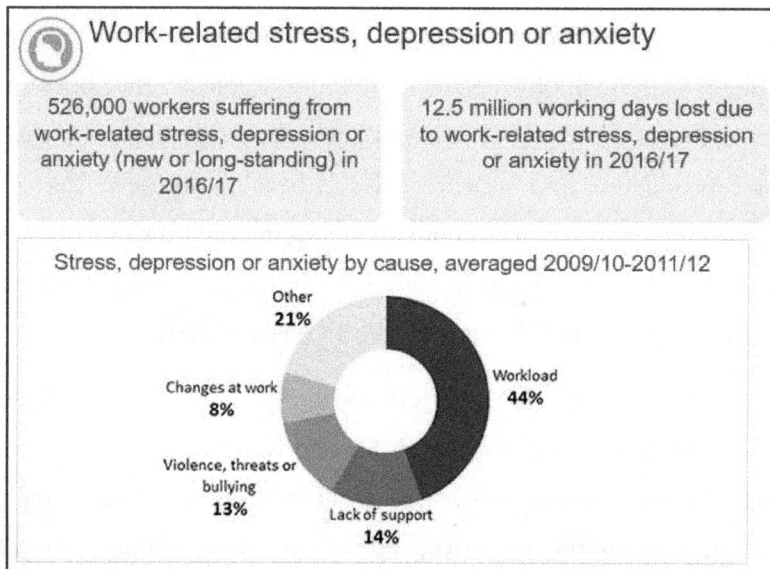

Source: http://www.hse.gov.uk/statistics/causdis/stress/index.htm

Psychological stressors are events we interpret as negative or threatening and can be socially induced. Some examples are being excluded from a group, death of a loved one, marital and financial problems. These difficulties all cause psychological stress.

Most physiological stressors are stressors to everyone, although the degree to which it is experience depends on the individual. For example, we all have an individual threshold to pain, so what is painful to you may only annoy me.

Psychological stressors are relative, meaning that not everyone interprets them as stressful or attributes the same level of stress. They are subjective stressors and result in different reactions in different people. For example, driving home from work in heavy traffic is a high stressor for some people, but for others it is just a 'normal' part of their daily commute.

There are three stages to stress as defined by Hungarian endocrinologist Hans Selye, one of the first to study it in the late 1940s. The first stage is the alarm stage or the fight-or-flight response. During this stage your brain sends emergency signals to your body in reaction to what it perceives as an imminent threat. The body mobilizes itself by prioritizing body functions towards maximizing survival.

The second stage is resistance where our bodies try to return to normal, countering the alarm stage. In this stage you start to feel better and the stress seemingly disappears. This is your body trying to counter the stressor by throwing you into a false sense of well-being. If it remains, your body cannot keep 'fooling' itself and you will find you are exhibiting other stress responses like losing sleep, being irritable, and lacking focus. At this point you enter the third stage which is exhaustion.

The exhaustion stage is the final stage of stress and results from your body fighting the stressor for an extended period. The body begins to shut down, unable to fight illness because it lacks the energy to activate the immune system. Fatigue becomes constant, you have anxiety, depression, and you may experience recurring body inflammation and infection.

The human body has evolved various mechanisms to deal with stress and when stress becomes too much to handle, the body will reveal it in some way. By listening to your body and being aware of these mechanisms, you can initiate actions that short-circuit negative bodily reactions and control the release of the stress hormone cortisol.

Uncertainty is the most dangerous stressor

Recent research, which was carried out by a team from several institutions in the UK and published in Nature Communications, confirmed uncertainty in humans is more stressful than knowing something bad will definitely happen (Berker, et al. 2016). The experiment they designed was set up to measure stress levels by simulating a high stress situation.

They took volunteers and had them play a computer game that required them to turn over rocks that might have snakes hidden under them. If they turned over a rock with a snake, they received a painful electric shock. Participants were motivated to figure out a pattern to the rocks, some logic that explained which rocks had snakes under them to avoid shock. What they didn't know was the researchers implemented an algorithm that made sure the level of uncertainty fluctuated and made it impossible to avoid the shock. (Berker, et al. 2016)

The results confirmed that when the probability of finding a snake under a rock was unknown, the levels of cortisol concentrations rose. The research is one of the only ones to document that uncertainty is a key driver of high levels of stress in humans (Berker, et al. 2016).

When you're in a situation of uncertainty, your dopamine delivery system is activate making you try harder. It has been found that sport players try harder when the likelihood of success is uncertain. If making a goal is certain or impossible, it is not as rewarding as a situation where making a goal is on the borderline of being possible. The same has been hypothesized about addictive gamblers. The rush doesn't come from a sure bet, but from unpredictable wins and this uncertainty drives the addiction. (Linnet, et al. 2012)

Bodily reaction to stress was a part of our evolutionary intent to survive. A situation required action even when we could not be certain of the outcome, and our body pumped the chemicals it needed to orchestrate a response. But the result is stress. It is an interesting footnote in the connection to evolution with the snake and rock experiment that those whose stress mirrored actual – not imaginary – levels of uncertainty had an edge in predicting which rocks had snakes under them (Berker, et al. 2016). Stress and cortisol can help us perform better, but only in the short term and at levels that do not cause us to shut down.

The brain hates to not be in control, which is one reason why uncertainty is so stressful. We admire people who are in control of their lives and wish for the same. We direct our neural resources towards trying to control what is uncontrollable, life.

Too often, we are the source of uncertainty for people whether that be at work or in our personal lives. We unwittingly, or even purposely, hold back information that would relieve their uncertainty. We don't consider how a few words, a response to an email or text message, or a frank conversation about what we're thinking, or planning might improve that person's life and help them avoid unnecessary stress.

Sometimes people think they are doing us a favor by not telling us bad news, but research shows us that not knowing the bad news creates higher stress than knowing it. It is far less stressful to know that something bad happened, a relationship is over, or a client doesn't want to continue working with you. For the brain, it has a finality about helping you to move on and look for other opportunities. When the door of possibility is kept open, the brain is left to wonder if it can change the situation to have a positive outcome. This is the situation that causes damaging levels of stress.

In my work I sell my services to organizations and maintain the customer relationship. I have had clients that are honest and direct in how they conduct their business with me. They tell me when they have problems, or when plans change, and we speak about the situation and agree on the next steps together. Those customers I appreciate and trust. I know that they will keep me informed and will answer my emails or return my phone calls. It might take them some days to do so, but I can be sure they will do it and I need not wonder or try again to contact them. This helps keep me from imagining worst-case scenarios which elevate my stress levels and risk my health.

The other side of the coin are clients who do not communicate at all. They do not answer emails, don't return my calls, and leave me to wonder what is going on and where things are with their business. I have had clients cancel training sessions with me and not inform me. Others have scheduled meetings and then not shown up, providing no excuse or explanation. I am left to wonder what happened and where things stand with a complete lack of information. This sends my stress levels through the roof and I have spent sleepless nights wondering what happened and why someone doesn't respond.

Some react this way because they believe they are undertaking impression management. They think by not telling me they do not wish to cooperate, or something has changed in the budget, I will not see them as the 'bad guy.' They just ignore me and hope I will go away, which is the basic fear response triggered by not wanting to experience the pain of what they perceive as disappointing me.

But when you behave this way you do not protect your image. The stress you cause in others can lead to negative consequences, even in the extreme, death from stress-induced heart attack. Remember social pain is interpreted by the brain as a close equivalent to physical pain. You wouldn't consider punching a person you work with in the face, so why would you consider leaving them wondering about their fate with your relationship? It is the same pain you are causing them.

Reducing uncertainty in others will help you build better relationships – ones built on the notion of trust, respect, and thoughtfulness. Science shows knowing bad news is better than not knowing at all. You should not fear giving bad news as the reaction is likely to be much less negative then what your brain fears.

Stress makes us stupid

Yes, you heard me right: stress makes us stupid.

I could say it in a more scientific way: stress impairs our cognitive ability, but I thought I would say it like this for all you who are now stressed out and have had their IQ lowered because of it. All jokes aside, the latest research supports that idea that when stressed, it has a negative impact on your IQ and cognitive abilities.

Research from neuroscience has now quantified the impact of stress on IQ. When your thinking ability gets impaired by high-stress situations and you find yourself overwhelmed, your IQ can drop by as much as 10-15 points. With the mean global IQ being around 90 (Global IQ: 1950–2050 n.d.), a 10 to 15-point drop is significant and worrying. A person with an IQ of below 75 is considered to be cognitively impaired.

There are many infamous examples of smart people in demanding, even life-threatening, situations unable to decide, freezing under stress. One example from recent history is of the failure of Japanese executives to respond with timely decisions in the wake of the 2011 magnitude 9.1 Tōhoku earthquake and subsequent tsunami, crippling the nuclear reactor at Fukushima. The indecision by the leadership at the Tokyo Electric Power Company (TEPCO) was a good example of how intelligent people caught in the stress and pressure of a situation, where every decision could cause the loss of a significant number of lives, just froze.

Prime Minister Naoto Kan asked from TEPCO executives handling the disaster why there was a delay in venting the reactor that would explode and result in a melt-down and the answer was: "I don't know." Naoto Kan explained in his testimony at the inquiry to the accident, "The answer – 'I don't know' – was troublesome. If we knew whether it was a technical matter or other reasons, we could figure out [a further step]" (Shinoda 2013). Faced with the possibility of making a decision that could have far-reaching negative consequences, the pressure caused the brain to stop blood flow to the S2 (prefrontal cortex) reducing the intelligence of those responsible for deciding how to avert the disaster.

Neurobiologist Amy Arnsten at Yale University School of Medicine found even mild acute uncontrollable stress can cause a rapid and dramatic loss of S2 prefrontal cognitive abilities. Prolonged stress can cause changes in the structure of our S2 prefrontal brain. (Arnsten 2009)

Some of the early studies related to stress and the effects on our cognitive abilities took place following World War II. The observation was made that highly skilled pilots often crashed their planes in the stress of battle due to mental errors. Researchers found exposure to high stress impaired our abilities for complex and flexible thinking. Interestingly, it found simpler, or well-rehearsed tasks improved in stress situations (Broadbent 1971). The improvement in simple tasks could be attributed to muscle memory, which is the ability to reproduce a movement without conscious thought, gained through repetition of movement, for example playing guitar or typing.

Any strong emotion – fear, stress, anxiety, anger, betrayal, even joy – will trigger the amygdala and impair the prefrontal cortex's ability to process memory. Emotion overwhelms rationality in these situations causing us to not 'think straight.' Our IQ is temporarily depleted and our S1 amygdala, now in survival mode can, and does, make you do things against your better judgment (Nadler 2011).

Stress reduction through altered brain networks

To reduce stress, we need to alter the brain's network. Throughout human history people have practiced various forms of meditation to rest the mind and attain a state of emotional calmness. It is not my goal in this book to describe the 'ideal' meditative practices, but to provide a view of what the neuroscience research tells us about how meditation changes our brains.

The University of Wisconsin at Madison studied the brain activity of people who practiced meditation. In one of the largest studies to date, covering over 150 adults, the University's Center for Healthy Minds used fMRI scans to look at the differences in brains of 3 groups, new meditators, non-meditators, and long-term meditators with thousands of hours of meditation practice (Tammi R.A. Kral 2018).

New-meditators were assigned to an eight-week course in mindfulness and stress reduction based in meditation practices. Non-meditators were the control group and were assigned to a general health enhancement program that included well-being practices, but no meditation. Long-term meditators were not given any new program but encouraged to carry on with their daily meditation routines.

After an eight-week period, participants were asked to view and label photos as either emotionally positive, negative or neutral while being scanned in an fMRI machine.

The results showed significantly reduced activity in the amygdala, the area of our brain critical to emotion, when the new and long-term meditators viewed emotionally positive images. However, the reduced amygdala activity for negative images was only prevalent in the long-term meditators, showing it may take more practice in meditation to modulate our reactions to negative emotions. (Tammi R.A. Kral 2018)

What is important about this study is that it is one of the first to connect meditation with functional changes in the underlying circuitry of our brain, even with as little as eight weeks of practice. The researchers observed an increase in connectivity between the amygdala and the prefrontal cortex in new meditators. Leading to the conclusion it is possible to control emotion with practice. However, even more interesting was the increase in connectivity was not observed in the long-term meditators' brains. The theory of why they didn't have increased connection was their ability to handle emotion was so advanced it had been moved to an S1 automated process. (Tammi R.A. Kral 2018)

Think what that means for the case of including meditation in your everyday life. Not only is it possible to control your emotions, but control of them might be moved to an automated, habitual, process. It could be described as a state of nirvana, which is the Buddhist concept of a transcendent state in which there is neither suffering, desire, nor sense of self.

To automate your response to emotion to where you are devoid of any stress from the process, might be one step in the attainment of nirvana. It is a more involved and complicated concept, but interesting to think neuroscience may help us attain it. However, before you get too excited that a short meditation course can lead to spiritual enlightenment, it must be stated that those who moved emotion to an automated process had 1 000s of hours of experience in meditation.

The University of Wisconsin's research also meshes well with Northeastern University's Lisa Feldman Barrett's research of constructed emotion. If emotions are constructed, then it is possible to construct them in a way which is more positive. Barrett argues in her book, *How Emotions Are Made* (Feldman Barrett n.d.), that we learn concepts like anger and disgust and they are not genetically pre-determined. If they are learned, then it is possible to alter the reaction to them by reframing them.

Part of most meditation practices is controlled breathing and there is direct evidence from neuroscience in the value of purposeful breathing.

In a 2016 study on mice, researchers accidentally discovered the neural circuit in the brainstem that appears to control the rhythm of breathing. A small, well-defined cluster of neurons in the breathing rhythm generator appears to regulate the balance in the brain between calm and arousal states. When researchers removed this bundle of cells, it left the mice unusually calm, signifying their function as a regulator of emotion. What is exciting about this finding is it connects for the first time that breathing can influence higher-order S2 brain function. (Kevin Yackle 2017)

A study involving humans also found that focus on breathing activated regions of the brain known for controlling emotion, memory and awareness. In the study published in 2018 in the Journal of Neurophysiology, researchers at the Interdepartmental Neuroscience Program and Kellogg School of Management at Northwestern University, had participants count how many breaths they took over a two-minute period, heightening their attention and focus to their breathing. When participants counted correctly the number of breaths taken, their brain activity showed a more organized pattern versus the pattern observe when they were resting (Herrero, et al. 2018). It confirms that controlling and focusing your breathing activates higher-order, S2, brain functions and provides a pathway to the control of emotions.

These studies suggest a new way of looking at how to deal with stress. Instead of focusing on strategies involving more sleep, exercise, a healthier diet, and an increase in time for family and friends, we should look at how to re-wire our brain circuitry. The research is showing it is possible, even with simple interventions, to control how our brain is connecting and what parts of it are being activated. With practice in focused attention it may be possible to wire the connections in the brain that promote positive outcomes and disconnect those that are ineffective or negative. The possibility for emotional self-regulation exists and perhaps with increased attention to understanding how to create better connections in our brains, it will be achieved.

The chemical of tend and befriend

One of the brain's most influential chemicals for developing social connections is oxytocin. Oxytocin is what spurs us to behaviors that support tend and befriend and away from fight, flight, or freeze.

Oxytocin was first discovered in 1906 by British pharmacologist Sir Henry Hallet Dale as the chemical that induced contractions in the uterus and for forming a maternal bond between mother and child. Oxytocin, the word, is derived from the Greek word 'oxys' (quick) and 'tokos' (birth) and is unique to mammals. Since its discovery, it has been found to be present also in males and plays a key role in social bonding.

"Oxytocin is a powerful hormone that acts as a neurotransmitter in the brain. It regulates social interaction and sexual reproduction, playing a role in behaviors from maternal-infant bonding and milk release to empathy, generosity, and orgasm. When we hug or kiss a loved one, oxytocin levels increase..." In fact, the hormone plays a huge role in all pair bonding. The hormone is greatly stimulated during sex, birth, and breastfeeding. Oxytocin is the hormone that underlies trust. It is also an antidote to depressive feelings." (Oxytocin Pair Bonding - Oxytocin Basics 2018)

Popular science has taken the latest neuroscience research proclaiming oxytocin as the 'love hormone' or the 'moral molecule.' But this simplification doesn't do justice to the important and far-reaching impact of this chemical on your life. Oxytocin makes the brain pay better attention to the social environment, using that improved awareness to create stronger bonds (Young 2018). It helps you to focus on others and process incoming stimuli to help determine the value of a social interaction.

In one study oxytocin was found to play a critical role as a catalyst to ignite our hippocampus, which manages memory formation. It was also found to play an important role in determining who is part of our preferred social group. As Harvard University neuroscientist Tara Raam explains:

"Our results indicate that oxytocin usurps this preexisting neural circuit within the hippocampus that normally regulates the differentiation of similar memories. In the presence of oxytocin, the circuit assumes an additional role as a regulator of social cognition." (Raam, et al. 2017)

Oxytocin, therefore, plays a part in determining if a person is a friend or foe, providing us with the intuitive memory of those who have harmed us, and those who have cared for us. In a landmark study, the first to link oxytocin to social stress, scientists at Northwestern University identified for the first time the pathway oxytocin uses to enhance negative emotions (previously it was thought that it was responsible only for positive emotions). (Radulovic and Tronson 2011)

It was found that oxytocin intensifies negative social memory and future anxiety by triggering an important signaling molecule. This molecule, ERK, becomes activated for six hours after a negative social experience. ERK enhances fear by stimulating the brain's fear pathways (Radulovic and Tronson 2011) .

When oxytocin is administered artificially via a nasal spray it has been shown to stimulate certain aspects of social interaction including eye gazing, the ability to correctly interpret facial expressions and vocal tones (Uvnäs-Moberg, K., Handlin, L., & Petersson, M. 2014).

Oxytocin and our significant other

We know that in love relationships there is a high level of oxytocin released between partners and that this is not only a sexually induced chemical attractor. In fact, research with prairie voles has shown that the bond between pairs is not a direct consequence of sexual attraction. Researchers were surprised to find that voles would pick a partner, live with that partner, and have multiple offspring with them, but when the researchers tried to get them to exhibit a sexual preference for their

Prairie Vole

familiar partner, they refused. According to Dr. C. Sue Carter, who was the first person to identify the physiological mechanisms responsible for monogamy, the bond created was something altogether deeper than just a sexual preference and attraction. The voles were 'socially monogamous' meaning a consistent social partner mattered more than who was providing the sperm. The voles care about who they live with and who helps to raise their offspring. (Ledford 2008)

A similar finding was found in research on humans. Oxytocin artificially administered to monogamous men caused them to avoid an attractive woman. It promoted stronger binding with their significant other and not with an attractive stranger (Scheele D 2012). In another study published in 2013, it was found that male subjects had an enhanced preference for their female partners when oxytocin was artificially administered. When subjects were given oxytocin, they rated their partner's faces as more attractive compared with unfamiliar women, and brain scans confirmed an activation of their reward system when viewing their partners (Scheele, et al. 2013).

These studies support the belief that although there is a reproductive cost for males, monogamy helped to ensure offspring survival. From an evolutionary perspective, it makes sense that oxytocin would be produced for this purpose. It ensured the survival of the species by the male providing more than just reproductive material.

Today you do not have species survival at stake in your bonding with others, but the brain continues to use these chemical neurotransmitters to influence your relationships. Societies around the globe are predominately monogamous. It has been theorized this was heavily influenced by Christianity, but it can well be humans are preprogrammed to be monogamous. The evidence one way or the other is not yet there to provide a definitive answer. We will have to wait for further research before it can be confirmed. Research into oxytocin indicates we bond strongly with significant others and when oxytocin levels remain high, we prefer to stay with them.

It is also interesting to note that couples in the first six months of a relationship have almost twice the levels of oxytocin as single people. Those couples exhibit more affection, such as touching and eye-gazing, and stay together longer (Schneiderman, et al. 2012). Part of the bonding process for long-term monogamy seems to be this strong initial connection when first together. Some might describe that feeling as 'love' which in fact may be the strong chemical bond we create when we recognize another as a suitable long-term companion.

Oxytocin and pets

French Briard Sheepdog

Oxytocin release is not confined to intraspecies release – it also occurs between humans and pets. One interesting finding has been that dogs produce oxytocin in a reciprocal loop with their human owners. Those of us that own dogs know well how attached we get to them and how much a part of our family they become. Researchers have found oxytocin is also at work in creating and strengthening the between dog and owner.

When humans look into the eyes of their dogs, researchers recorded an oxytocin spike, and when dogs were artificially given oxytocin they looked more into the eyes of their owners. This creates a continues feedback loop that provides a strong bond. (Petersson, et al. 2017)

However, if we look at the dog's ancestor, the wolf, they do not look into humans' eyes and oxytocin is not released. During the domestication of dogs, we have selected dogs that engage in eye contact and facilitate the release of oxytocin and this serves as a chemical mechanism that binds us together. The dog was an important partner to humans for thousands of years and oxytocin supported that relationship. (Petersson, et al. 2017)

Pets can be an excellent addition to environments that can benefit from oxytocin release. I know of one CEO of a Helsinki-based mobile game company who brings his dog to work daily. The dog is affectionately looked after by the employees and through the stimulated release of oxytocin, helps to forge closer bonds in the team. When oxytocin is present, no matter what the source of its creation, it works to connect people and build higher levels of trust. It is not surprising that people describe the company culture as a 'family.'

The role of oxytocin in modern social bonding

The role of oxytocin in forming bonds is an important evolutionary development and has a direct connection to your day-to-day life. It is not just with your children, significant others, or pets where we use oxytocin release to connect. You also use it with close friends and in close working relationships, our 'in-group.' Your in-group is people who are in your close social circle. You can think of them as your tribe.

Understanding what triggers oxytocin production and using it to create stronger bonds with others, is one of the remarkable findings that has come out of neuroscience research in recent years. You can cultivate the production of oxytocin to stimulate oxytocin neuroreceptors and use it to create stronger social bonds with others.

Skin is the largest organ of the body, measuring more than two square meters if laid flat, and is the pathway for touch. Touch is the most powerful and important functions we have in creating strong social bonds. Researchers at Oxford's Center for Computational Neuroscience have been using fMRI machines to study touch and its impact on human behavior. What they found is pleasant touch activates the brain's orbitofrontal cortex, that area of our brain responsible for reward and decision making. (Rolls 2016)

Pleasant touch is what is important to the release of oxytocin and is defined as having moderate pressure, according to the Touch Research Institute at the University of Miami School of Medicine. This is why a firm handshake, executed with moderate pressure, is better than a flimsy handshake or one that is crushing (Bucci 2018). When we experience appropriate touch oxytocin release puts our mind into a state of calm, receptive to connection, and trust of others.

Oxytocin release requires the expenditure of energy. Before your brain decides to release oxytocin, it must decide that the cost of doing so is worthwhile. In order to release oxytocin from touch, the connection needs to last between six and 20 seconds and needs to be from a person you know and want to engage in touch with. Unwanted touch from a stranger or even someone we know, does not release oxytocin. A quick handshake or pat on the back is also unlikely to be enough to convince the brain to spend the energy.

It is important to note that the half-life of oxytocin in the circulation of humans is 30 minutes. It is short-lived, but the connection that is formed can be long-lasting (Groot, et al. 1995). It is even thought that touch is as vital to our long-term well-being as food and security.

If you don't have someone to hug, then a pet can also work as a good substitute, remember that your dog also produces oxytocin. Even a bit of self-massage can help to release it, although it is not as effective as touch from others. Other ways include giving someone a gift (in the following sections we will discuss in more detail gratitude), talking with friends (even over social media), practicing yoga or mindfulness, and getting warm, perhaps by sitting on the beach or in front of a fire. There are even some negative self-soothing behaviors such as smoking and stress eating that increase oxytocin.

A question that might come to mind is why don't we all just take oxytocin supplements? The reason is that oxytocin degrades quickly at room temperature. Even in studies, it needed to be given either intravenously or with heavy nasal doses – more than three teaspoons worth. For this reason, at least at this time, it is not practical to think we can just pop a pill and get the benefits.

Oxytocin and work relationships

One pioneer in the field of oxytocin benefits is Dr. Paul Zak who is founding Director of the Center for Neuroeconomics Studies. Zak's groundbreaking discovery was the role oxytocin played in forming and maintaining trustful relations.

If you ask people who they trust in their lives the universal response will be their family. The trust you have with a member of your immediate family is strong. Oxytocin plays an important part in establishing and maintaining that trust. We saw earlier how oxytocin played a part in establishing the bond between mother and child and how it helped to support monogamous relationships. What Zak found was that we can also create high-trust, oxytocin-induced relationships with others, including with those we work with, if we cultivate the relationships. (Zak, The neuroscience of high-trust organizations. 2018)

Research into oxytocin has established that it increases the time we spend gazing at others' faces and helps in our recognition of people, the stronger the oxytocin release the better we can recall people and interpret their emotions and intentions (G. Domes 2007). Research has also discovered that oxytocin helps to produce the 'I want to help' effect in others and increases our empathetic concerns (Paul J Zak 2013).

Zak and his colleague Jorge Barraza came up with the first mathematical derivation of trust that arises from voluntary cooperation and showed how it affects economic performance (Paul J Zak 2013). They found that that oxytocin infusions into humans via nasal administered spray increased the level of trust even among persons who are complete strangers. When oxytocin was given artificially to persons taking part in a trust game, they showed a much higher rate of trust than those on a placebo (45% vs. 22%). His studies provide evidence that oxytocin helps us to determine who to trust and when to reciprocate it (Michael Kosfeld 2005). Artificially administered oxytocin was found to promote a host of other positive social behaviors including generosity and charity (Paul J Zak 2013).

Trust the cornerstone of psychological safety

The importance of trust in working relationships cannot be overstated and forms the cornerstone of psychologically safe workplaces. Organizational behavioral scientist Amy Edmondson of Harvard University is one of the leading researchers in the field of psychological safety. Edmondson coined the concept of psychological safety and defines it as "a shared belief that a team is safe for personal risk-taking... that the team will not embarrass, reject or punish someone for speaking up." (Edmondson 1999). Furthermore, psychologically safe environments facilitate the willing contribution of ideas and actions to a shared enterprise and helps to explain why employees share information and knowledge, speak up with suggestions for improvements, and take initiative to develop new products and services.

Edmondson built on the work of William Kahn who observed that psychological safety enables personal engagement at work. It facilitates a willingness to employ or express themselves physically, cognitively, and emotionally rather than disengage or withdraw and defend their personal selves. Further, Kahn argued that people are more likely to believe they will be given the benefit of the doubt – a defining characteristic of psychological safety – when relationships within a given group are characterized by trust and respect. (Kahn 1990)

Testosterone's impact on oxytocin

Testosterone, the predominately male sex hormone – although women also produce it at lower levels – is widely known for fueling aggression. High levels of testosterone have been shown to lower empathy. Paul Zak's lab found when testosterone levels were high in men, they were 27% less generous towards strangers and even used their position to punish those who were ungenerous towards them (Paul J. Zak 2009).

Another study conducted by Utrecht University discovered, through fMRI scans, the region of the brain responsible for empathy was interrupted by testosterone. Researchers artificially administered a single dose of testosterone to 16 young women (elevating their testosterone levels by a factor of 10) and had them take the "Reading the Mind in Eyes Test" (RMET), a well-known test for measuring social intelligence (Bos, et al. 2016).

The researchers found the ability of the participants to accurately assess the emotional state of people took longer. The results show that testosterone impairs cognitive empathy, preventing the ability to understand the emotions of others (Bos, et al. 2016).

In a third study published in 2015 researchers found an interesting connection between testosterone, cortisol, and empathy. Participants (women and men) took the RMET and the Interpersonal Reactivity Index (IRI) questionnaire designed to measure aspects of empathy. What they found was a direct correlation between high levels of testosterone and a lack of empathy. However, when participants had a high level of cortisol (the stress hormone) and high testosterone empathy increased. (Zilioli, et al. 2015)

The implications for work are far-reaching. People who are given social power and have high levels of testosterone show an increase in entitlement and reduced empathy. This is not just a male phenomenon, but also found in females in positions of power. Nicole Mead, research head, states:

"Those effects occur only among those with relatively high testosterone. So, women who have high testosterone for women act no differently from high-testosterone men. Statistically, I standardized (sic) testosterone within men and women separately. Gender did not play a role in this study." (Mead 2018)

Not everyone who is in a position of power exhibits a lack of empathy, but there are many who do. For organizations who need high-functioning teams built on trust and psychological safety to perform optimally, lack of empathy is a crucial problem. According to Paul Zak:

"Compared with employees at low-trust organizations, the high-trust folks had 11% more empathy for their workmates, depersonalized them 41% less often, and experienced 40% less burnout from their work. They felt a greater sense of accomplishment, as well—41% more." (Zak, The Neuroscience of Trust 2017)

The need to be reminded that power can lower chemically the ability to empathize with others is important to mitigating the negative impact. In Paul Zak's book, The Trust Factor, he tells how Michael Dell had a problem with a negative image and people not wanting to work with him. In one assessment it was found most people at Dell did not want to work with him and, if given the opportunity, would quit and go to work elsewhere. Michael Dell turned the situation around by hiring a coach and putting triggers to remind himself of his negative social tendencies, like the plastic bulldozer on his desk that reminded him to not 'run over' people (Zak, Trust Factor: The Science of Creating High-Performance Companies 2017). It is a striking example of what can happen if you let testosterone overtake your brain and direct actions that go against creating a strong and trusting culture.

Oxytocin is not purely positive

There are profound benefits of promoting oxytocin with those both in our private and professional lives. However, oxytocin also has a dark side and if you amplify it too much it can give rise to emotions that trigger negative behavior. As Dr. Loretta Graziano Breuning, founder of the Inner Mammal Institute explains, "In the state of nature, lowered vigilance can bring lethal harm, so the mammal brain is careful about when it releases oxytocin." It strengthens the bond with our 'tribe,' our family and close co-workers, but it also makes us more protective of those in our group. Think of a mother protecting her children and you appreciate the power of oxytocin to make us protective. (Breuning 2012)

The protective nature of oxytocin can be a positive thing in an organization. It can be used to fend off competition and rally people around a business threat, so it can be a powerful and positive influencer. But research warns that if the levels of oxytocin are too high it can have negative consequences.

When people are exceedingly protective, people can resort to lies and ignore ethics if they believe it will benefit the group. The Volkswagen emissions scandal of 2015 is perhaps an example of oxytocin levels in a group raised to a level where members bent the rules, resulting in several arrests and some imprisonments. Studies have found that people given high doses of oxytocin were twice as likely to lie as those with normal levels (Shalvia and De Dreu 2014). Engineers in the emissions control department may have thought bending the rules was a way to protect the company and their market position.

Other studies have found too much oxytocin creates walls between you and those not in your tribe by intensifying fear and mistrust towards outsiders. It can even fuel feelings of prejudice, envy, aggression, and xenophobia, and diminish collaboration among groups within an organization (Carsten K. W. De Dreu 2011). Oxytocin appears to intensify feelings that lead us to view harshly and negatively those not considered a part of our inner group.

In another study from the University of Haifa in Israel, neuroscientists gave high doses of oxytocin to participants who were playing a game of chance. Participants on oxytocin reported increased levels of envy or gloating when they lost or won money in a controlled game compared to a placebo group. The researchers concluded that oxytocin promotes higher intensity of social emotions leading to more generosity and trust in positive contexts but, disturbingly, more envy and gloat in competitive situations. (Simone G. Shamay-Tsoory 2009)

The research on oxytocin continues and certainly will yield additional insights in the future. It is one chemical having great impact on your social interactions, how you interpret the intentions of others, and whether you bond or push people away. Much of how you behave is tied to the hormones being released in your brain. The better your understanding of the influence of these hormones, the easier it is for you to control them and direct your actions towards a positive outcome.

Understanding the negative influence these hormones have on driving your behavior should give you pause. Learning to move emotion to your prefrontal cortex (S2) where it can be processed is how we learn to be less reactive and develop better self-control. It is how we break away from being a slave to our hormones.

When I realized how hormones were negatively influencing my own behavior and pushing me towards reactions that were based on fear, it was a huge revelation. I reflected on some of the interactions I had in the past and realized how they were reactions to situations where my brain delivered a fearful emotion and I reacted by trying to protect myself. I still struggle with this and fight my brain daily. Being an entrepreneur is fraught with uncertainty and stress. It takes being constant vigilance to control the emotions and processes them into feelings where they can be evaluated and disregarded if they do not support a positive agenda.

Sometimes you see people react in an out of line, perplexing way. When you understand they are reacting to their hormones, you can have more empathy for them. You can also help to dispel their fears by adjusting your own behavior and controlling your reactions. People's behavior is never random. They are reacting off emotion triggered by stimuli which constructs feelings of threat to their well-being or safety.

In my coaching work I always tell people that one of the hardest things to argue with, or get angry at, is empathy. No one can fault you for being understanding of the problems they are facing, or the emotions they feel. You do not have to agree with them, you only have to empathize and show you can understand what they are feeling. Often, the anger and difficulties melt away and the person moves into a more agreeable state of calm. Empathy is a powerful tool for managing emotions.

When we understand the chemical drivers to behavior, it is easier to move to our logical S2 brain and process it rather than reacting to it. Your brain will fight you in this process as it prefers to act on emotion. Pittsburgh Pirate baseball manager Chuck Tanner once said; "There are three secrets to managing. The first secret is to have patience. The second is be patient. And the third most important secret is patience" (McCollister 2005).

This also applies to managing your brain. It takes constant effort to control your behavior and understand others' actions. Your brain will fight you and encourage you, like the devil on your shoulder whispering in your ear, to be reactive. Exert your dominance over your lazy brain and take control, and you will be rewarded.

The power of mirror neurons to drive relationships

The brain has a native ability to replay and remember events in vivid detail, but what is also incredible about the brain is its ability to feel and experience the emotions of others through thought. Imagine you are watching a basketball game on TV and the ball ricochets off the backboard and hits a player square in the face. Most of us watching this recoil and moan in sympathy. Or you are watching a football match and a brilliant play results in a touchdown just as time is running out. You feel your heart race and your fist flies into the air. These are examples of the brain's ability to 'mirror' the feelings of others and it is one of the most powerful social abilities of humans.

Mirror neurons were first discovered by a team of Italian researchers at the University of Parma in the late 80s early 90s led by neuroscientist Giacomo Rizzolatti. Rizzolatti and his colleagues studied macaque monkeys and the areas of their brains that were being triggered by certain actions. During their studies they found that not only did the brain 'light up' when doing an action themselves, but it also lit up when observing someone else doing that thing.

The initial observation was made by chance when a researcher picked up a piece of food as the macaque monkey's brain was wired for observation. The system recorded the monkey's brain reacting identically as when it picked up the food. Further studies showed 10% of

Macaque Monkey

the neurons in certain areas of the monkey's brain had 'mirror' properties which gave similar responses to performed hand actions and observed actions.

The identification of mirror neurons in monkeys led to a search for similar cells in humans. Experiments on monkey's involved invasive procedures of attaching electrodes directly to areas of the brain, which was not possible in humans. Instead, human trials focused on motor responses to observations of similar actions. When your brain invested in observations of activities, such as watching football, your muscles show signals indicating you are ready to move. The brain is processing the watched action as if we were doing it yourself. Rizzolatti was the first to record this phenomenon in humans and published his work in the Journal of Neurophysiology in 1995 (Giacomo Rizzolatti 1995).

In 1999, neuroscientists at the University of California at Los Angeles used the fMRI machine to image the brain activity of humans as they watched people making finger movements and repeating those movements themselves. What they observed in the brain scans was that the same areas in the frontal cortex and parietal lobule of the brain where active when doing as watching (M. Iacoboni 1999).

The existence of mirror neurons brings up several interesting questions about how humans perceive emotions in others. Professor Vittorio Gallese of the University of Parma was part of the team that discovered mirror neurons and has been active in researching their connection to embodied simulation theory.

Embodied simulation theory is a theory of how humans can understand others' actions, basic intentions and sensations. Gallese theorized it is the activation of the mirror neuron system that provides our basis of the experiential understanding of others' actions. This ability was responsible for allowing humans to thrive in complex social situations. Mirror neurons help us to understand the meaning of the actions and emotions of others simply by replicating them in our minds. (V Gallese 2004)

This is a profound discovery for and at the root of what makes you a social being. Gallese argues humans are wired for social connections from birth and by default see others as more similar than different. You are not, as previously thought, taught social behavior, but your brain is wired to be social from day one. This social wiring includes the amazing ability to recreate in the brain the emotions of others.

You can understand the power of this ability by watching an emotionally charged movie. Your brain understands that you are watching a movie, and what you are watching is not real, but your brain can process the emotions as though you were directly experiencing them. You cry, laugh, and your heart aches. It is the mirror neurons at work which allow you to feel what the character is doing on screen by recreating it in your brain.

It is important to realize it is not your prefrontal cortex reflecting on what has been seen and then constructing emotion to it. This would be too slow and just would not have the same result of feeling what the other person is feeling. The mirror neurons are using our S1 brains to rapidly recreate what you are seeing. When you see an Olympic weightlifter lift a heavy set of barbells, you are doing the same in your minds. You see Rocky taking a hard punch in the ring and you feel them landing on your body. It is an example of the brain's embodied simulation.

The importance of this understanding of how your brain simulates, is the realization that everything we do is one body responding to another. As Gallese puts it:

"One can only know the world through the body. In anything we are doing, whether walking on the beach or speaking to someone or studying a monkey, one is a body responding to another body. The relation is perpetually circular: a reciprocity of body to body. That is our phenomenological relation to the world—you can't get around it. One can never have a 'neutral scientific stance' of observation outside of this relation." (Badt 2013)

You are bound to your brain's ability to experience what others are experiencing and to use that ability to better interpret and understand those you interact with. It is an inbuilt ability and one used heavily each day.

One reason that storytelling has been touted as an important skill in motivating and leading people is because of our mirror neuron abilities. If you can experience through story what another has experienced, the connection established is more remarkable. It is bond made on a brain level. Research confirms when you are in sync with another's thinking, not only are you agreeing with them, but your brain is firing together with theirs in a similar manner.

Princeton professor of psychology and neuroscience Uri Hasson has been researching what happens in our brains during verbal communications. What he found was when we listen to other people telling a story about an event, our brains light up in a similar way as if we were viewing that event ourselves.

Dr. Hasson's team had people watch a clip from an episode of the BBC's drama Sherlock (a modern interpretation of the Sherlock Holmes detective) and then describe, or tell a story, of what happened, to another person. What Uri found was the brain scans from the fMRI studies were incredibly similar between those who watched the clip and those who heard the story of the clip. The listener's brain was a mirror of the speaker's brain. (Uri Hasson 2010)

However, just because you tell a story about an experience does not guarantee that the listener will understand it in the same way. Miscommunication plagues all of us. Dr. Hasson explains, you might 'hear' the same sound but because you lack the same embedded experience it can easily result in misinterpretation (Uri Hasson 2010).

For example, take the case of a Londoner hearing the words 'hackney carriage.' For a native of London this is recognizable as the city's iconic black cabs, but to a New Yorker the same phrase may hold no meaning. This is where the filters of our brain come into play. Remember we compare new experiences against those already stored in our memory to make quick sense of the new experience. The stored experience for a Londoner will have the words and a direct association for 'hackney carriage' but not necessarily for a New Yorker, especially one completely unfamiliar with London. (Hobson 2018)

To study this phenomenon of misinterpretation Hobson designed an experiment to pre-load experiences into the brains of participants and scan for differences. He had them read an abridged version of J.D. Salinger's *Pretty Mouth and Green My Eyes*, in which a husband loses his wife at a party and calls a friend to inquire if he has seen her. For one group he told them the wife was having an affair with the friend, and the other the husband was unreasonably jealous. What he found from brain scans was although scans were similar among group members, they were distinctly different between groups. The conclusion being the "differences in people's beliefs can substantially impact their interpretation of a series of events." (Yaara Yeshurun 2017)

People see the world through their own unique lens. No matter how we try to get them in sync with us through impassioned persuasion, the embedded experience that preexist in their brains will always be a difficult obstacle to overcome. We see this at play in the news media today with the increasingly polarization of political opinion. The popular news media is increasingly presenting only a single view through a single lens, reinforcing views rather than challenging them.

So how do we get brains out of sync and into sync if we are viewing the world from different perspectives? The key is in improving our conversational intelligence.

Conversational intelligence the key to brain synchronization

One of the first authors to inspire me with her work on understanding and applying neuroscience to relationships was Judith E. Glaser. Today I am privileged to call her a friend. Judith's work has centered on understanding better conversations and the role they play in developing the relationships we have.

Each day our lives are filled with a myriad of conversations. Those conversations determine how we connect or disconnect with others and are at the foundation of trustful relationships. When done correctly, those conversations allow us to engage in what Judith refers to as 'WE-centric' behaviors.

WE-centric behavior allows you to work with others, learn from each other, push the limits of innovation and creativity to accomplish more, together. When you develop your 'conversational intelligence' ability you learn to use the power of conversations to positively engage with others.

Judith explains in her best-selling book, *Conversational Intelligence* (Glaser 2013), conversations have three-dimensions, biochemical, relational, and co-creational. The biochemical side of a conversation is the hormonal dimension. We know our S1 brain handles the first interpretation of the contact we have with another person. If our perception triggers us to feel angry, guilty, anxious, or provoked, our body releases the hormone cortisol, which triggers a fear response in our S1 brain. When a fear response is triggered it blocks the flow of blood to your cognitive, prefrontal cortex S2 brain, and you are left in a state of uncontrolled emotional reaction.

The negative feelings towards those who triggered the response may get expressed as bullying, intimidation, and micromanaging. Those emotions can help to relieve your anger and disappointment but will also shut down the possibility for positive, co-creative, conversations. Your emotionally driven, S1 lizard brain, response is to erect a barrier cutting off the blood supply to your S2 brain making healthy conversations impossible. By recognizing when you are creating a barrier to conversational intelligence, you can move it to your S2 brain and work to reframe, refocus and redirect it towards positive outcomes.

Reframing asks you to take a difficult situation and turn it into an opportunity by finding a 'silver lining.' The brain's predominance for negative thinking is well established. Too often we get stuck in looking only at what might go wrong, or will not work, rather than opportunities and possibilities. Forcing your brain to reframe the idea by looking at it another way can raise your conversational intelligence.

One technique I like for reframing comes from Hal Gregersen, Executive Director of the MIT Leadership Center. Hal stumbled on a brainstorming technique with one of his MBA classes that forces the brain to reframe problems. Instead of brainstorming for answers, Hal turned his students thinking around by asking them to brainstorm for questions. By asking them to focus on coming up with as many questions as possible to a problem, rather than as many answers, it required the brain to consider the problem from another viewpoint (Gregersen 2018).

Refocusing allows you to move your attention from a narrow view to larger view. It is common to get stuck in a problem because it is too narrowly defined. When you take a step back and look from an expanded view it provides insight. Often, we get stuck in our own definition of a problem and this prevents us from hearing how others see it. By suspending judgment and letting others express how they view it, you can open your mind to new interpretations.

Suspending judgment and listening to others is one of the most difficult tasks you can undertake. It is not as simple as closing your mouth and not speaking, it is about stopping your mind from its constant search for what's next. Next time you are having an argument with someone, think about what your brain is doing. Are you listening, or are you planning your response to what the other person is saying? Stopping your brain from all the time searching for how to respond and what you should say and do next is difficult and takes self-control (something we know the brain hates).

Active listening is the skill for listening to another person to understand their view. To actively listen you must quiet your mind and focus your energy to your S2 brain by putting it to work. Take notes, reframe from interrupting, don't impose your views, thank them for their opinions, and repeat back your understanding, are techniques that promote active listening.

Listening is critical to developing conversational intelligence and building trust. I recently have been working on a trust measuring and building program with a young, progressive, IT company. As part of my work, the leadership management, consisting of nine persons, they took a trust-based 360 assessment (developed by neuroscientist Paul J. Zak). In the free comments for 'areas to improve,' 12 out of 43 comments expressed a need to listen more, that is 30% of the comments. I experienced this lack of listening in my interactions with people there. The CEO started to write an email in the middle of my sales presentation and the CCO (Chief Culture Officer) in subsequent meetings rarely let me complete a sentence before interrupting me.

Overall this company scores high in trust, but listening is a problem and has the potential to do great damage if left unchecked. Leaders and managers are programmed to give answers, and that goes against what you should be doing, which is listening.

Redirecting is another process for turning a negative conversation around by freeing yourself from an emotionally charged position. Judith talks in her book, *Conversational Intelligence* (Glaser 2013), about being addicted to being right. You can get a dopamine rush when arguing with other people and you are proven right and they are proven wrong. The rush of power and euphoria that you can get from this experience can become highly addictive with negative consequence.

In the workplace people will fall into a pattern of behavior where they argue positions continually until others give in and submit to them. It is even possible that people who develop this as a bad habit will find that being right no longer factors into their behavior. They will become unreasonable and even illogical in their thinking. What matters is the pleasure derived from being proven right and the associated dopamine rush.

As with breaking any bad habit, this one requires redirecting the brain in these situations to get unstuck from a limiting position. When interacting with people who have this habit it is first important to stop the argument by extracting yourself from the conversation. The best way to do this is to use empathy. It is nearly impossible to argue with a person who is empathetic towards you and it will have the effect of stopping their relentless pursuit of their dopamine fix. From there it takes patience to explain to them how their brain is negatively directing their actions. If you can get them to take a pause and reflect, it will be the first step towards helping them to break their habit. From there it will take constant work to help them to quiet their brains and break their addiction and move away from 'I' centric behaviors and towards 'WE' centric ones which hold greater possibilities.

The second dimension of conversations is relational. We are most comfortable when we are connected to others, sharing our ambitions, our dreams, and the stories of our lives. Social connection is a need deep within us.

Neuroscience has shown that we are so wired to social connection that our brains interpret social pain, being socially rejected or ostracized by others, shows up the same as physical pain (Novembre, Zanon and Silani 2015). When you connect with others on a relational level, they become part of an essential network that aids you in fulfilling your need to validate publicly your aspirations.

The third dimension is co-creational and is at the foundation of healthy and productive relationships. When we co-create, we are creating together a new reality incorporating the contributions of others. You move from 'I-centric' behaviors where you are more concerned with being proven right to 'WE-centric' behaviors where you suspend judgment, listen, and accept others' opinions as valued and necessary to your own success. WE centric behavior is where the potential exists for innovation and creativity, where breakthroughs happen, and purpose is realized.

Gratitude's Role in living better

Neuroscience has also opened the door to several fascinating insights into how the brain is affected by your outlook on life. The University of California has done several studies on the practice of showing gratitude and how it relates to well-being and improved cognitive ability.

First, we need to define what gratitude is. The definition of gratitude gets complex as there are many, but I will try to keep to the simpler definitions and the ones researchers use as a foundation for studies.

Gratitude is an emotion that promotes cooperative relationships and is experienced when an act reveals a person values the recipient by providing a benefit greater than what was expected (Forster, et al. 2017). Psychologist define it as a social emotion that signals our recognition of the thing's others have done for us (Glenn R. Fox 2015). The two elements important to feel gratitude are, first, the benefit must be unexpected, and second, it must be greater than what you expected. These two elements trigger in your brain the emotion we interpret as gratitude.

We can think of gratitude as a vehicle for forming and strengthening social connections. Charles Darwin theorized that gratitude may be a universally experienced emotion. Darwin in *The Descent of Man* observed humans are a profoundly social and caring species. Darwin argued your tendency towards sympathy is instinctual, hardwired into your brain, and even stronger than your instinct for self-preservation.

Gratitude played a part in our pre-historic past where our lives depended on the kindness of others. The demonstration of gratitude triggered the reward path in the brain providing a boost of dopamine to the person delivering a reward. The reward reinforced the social responsibility of others for helping one another, improving our chances of survival. (Trivers 1971)

Dr. Glen Fox, a leading researcher into gratitude from the University of California, looked at simple acts of gratitude such as holding a door open for another person, to giving another person a kidney or saving a person from the Nazis. Using fMRI scanners to view people's brains while they were experiencing gratitude, Fox sought to pinpoint the brain functions common to the emotion in both simple acts and those of profound importance. (Glenn R. Fox 2015)

Previously it was thought that gratitude was simply the emotion of receiving a nice thing, but what Fox's team revealed is it is more complex. fMRI scans showed grateful brains had increased activity in several areas including those responsible for; emotional processing, interpersonal bonding, social interactions, moral judgment, and the ability to understand the mental states of others (Glenn R. Fox 2015). Taken together those activities could be defined as the functions responsible for emotional intelligence, or your ability to read the emotions of others. Fox's work shows when the brain experiences gratitude it activates to make you more socially aware.

Research has also shown when receiving an unexpected act of kindness, you are inclined to return it in the future. This act of reciprocity has been studied and shown to be a part of the lives of our closest relatives, chimpanzees. In one study chimps were given a task requiring them to cooperate to get food. The hypothesis was that the chimps would be more willing to help friends or cooperate with those that were best at solving the problem. However, what was found was they were more likely to help those who had earlier helped them. Reciprocity appeared to be more important than friendship or skill (Malini Suchak 2016). The same was observed in experiments on humans.

At Baylor University, researchers had a group of participants play a game where they were to distribute money between each other. Over a series of rounds participants were delivered money a partner had gifted to them. However, unbeknown to participants, researchers assigned each randomly to one of two groups. In group 1 they were told their partner had given them $9 and kept just $1, and were given a handwritten note that read, "I saw that you didn't get a lot in the last round that must've been a bummer." In the second group participants were told they received $9 by chance with their partner getting $1. They received no note. (Tsang 2006)

When interviewing the participants at the end of the experiment, those that got the note reported being more motivated to reciprocate the favor. They also returned the favor more in following rounds, giving more money back, than those who believed they got the money by chance. "Grateful feelings motivated the individual to act prosocially (sic) towards his or her original benefactor" (Tsang 2006). The finding shows grateful emotions help to establish and reinforce reciprocal relationships where favors and privileges are interchanged between individuals.

The research appears to confirm the 'Golden Rule,' "Do unto others as you would have them do unto you," which has existed for thousands of years and can be found in nearly every major religion. It is not surprising we find this idea throughout all civilizations. The human brain is wired to seek and provide benefits to those who show kindness to us.

Side note: some of the formulations of the Golden Rule from various religions:

✓ Baha'i: Choose thou for thy neighbor that which thou choosest for thyself. —Lawh'i 'Ibn'i Dhib, "Epistle to the Son of the Wolf" 30

✓ Brahmanism: This is the sum of duty: do naught unto others which would cause you pain if done to you. —Mahabharata 5:1517

✓ Buddhism (560 BCE): Hurt not others with that which pains yourself. —Udana-Varga 5.18

✓ Confucianism: Do not do to others what you do not want done to yourself. —Analects 15:23

✓ Egypt (2000 BC): Do for one who may do for you, that you may cause him thus to do. —The Eloquent Peasant

✓ Greece (400 BCE): Do not do to others what would anger you if done to you by others. —Socrates

✓ Hinduism (3200 BCE): One should always treat others as they themselves wish to be treated. —The Hitopadesa

✓ Islam: Not one of you is a believer until you wish for others what you wish for yourself." —Fortieth Hadith of an-Nawawi 13

✓ Jainism: One should treat all creatures in the world as one would like to be treated." —Sutrakritanga 1:11:33

✓ Judaism (1300 BCE): Thou shalt love thy neighbor as thyself. —Leviticus 19:18

✓ Sikhism: Treat others as thou wouldst be treated thyself. —Adi Granth

✓ Taoism: Regard your neighbor's gain as our own gain, and your neighbor's loss as your own loss. —T'ai Shang Kan Ying P'ien

✓ Zoroastrianism (600 BCE): That nature alone is good which refrains from doing unto another whatsoever is not good for itself. —Dadistan-I-Dinik, 94:5

(M. Morris 2012)

Benefits of Practicing Gratitude

Learning to be grateful, celebrate the things we have, and appreciate the every day 'gifts' others contribute to our lives is something research shows has many positive health and well-being benefits.

One of the key benefits of practicing gratitude includes reducing the stress hormone cortisol and increasing oxytocin. The combined effect promotes healthier and more meaningful relationships. In a 2015 study, researchers found that thanking a new acquaintance makes them more likely to seek an ongoing relationship (Williams and Bartlett 2015). The researchers' findings for the first time support the evidence that perceptions of interpersonal warmth, friendliness, and thoughtfulness, serve as mechanisms via which gratitude connects and advances your connection to others.

A 2012 study found those who rate high in gratitude were more empathetic and showed less aggressive tendencies. Participants in the study who had been identified as high-grateful persons were more likely to behave in a prosocial manner. They showed overall more sympathy and sensitivity towards other people and a decreased desire to seek reprisal (DeWall, et al. 2012).

The benefits of good sleep to human health is well documented and research has shown that practicing gratitude will help improve sleep. In a 2009 study involving 400 adults, of all ages, showed those who spent just 15 minutes jotting down things they were grateful for before going to bed reported sleeping better and longer and needing less time to fall asleep. Participants also had a carry-over of thankful thinking to the next day and had less daytime dysfunction. (Wood, Joseph, Lloyd, & Atkins, 2009)

Another study published in 2016, involving 119 young well-educated women, asked participants to keep a simple diary recording what they were grateful for. The results not only showed increases in optimism and sleep quality, but also reductions in blood pressure and an increase in overall well-being (Jackowska, et al. 2016).

Neuroscience has also shown keeping a gratitude journal is beneficial to the brain (Kini 2016) (Karns, Moore and Mayr 2017). A 2016 fMRI imaging study published in the *Frontiers in Human Neuroscience* confirmed participants who wrote a daily gratitude journal, experienced a change to their S2 brains. Those who took part in a program were required to reflect daily on the things they were grateful for. In just three weeks changes to the ventromedial prefrontal cortex (vmPFC), the area responsible for social decision making, were documented. The participants expressed feeling more generosity and selflessness towards others during the time they were keeping the journal. Researcher Christine Karns commented that the study "suggests that there's more good out there when there is gratitude." (University of Oregon 2017)

Journaling does not have to be a tedious task, a simple listing of three things you are grateful for each night before bed is a great start and produces benefits. For me growing up in a Christian family in the mid-West I said my prayers each night, and part of those prayers was giving thanks for those people in my life.

For those not into journaling or prayer, Dr. Glenn Foxx, Research Fellow at USC's Brain and Creativity Institute, recommends spending a few moments each day contemplating things in your life you appreciate. He explains, in the morning he takes a moment to contemplate the small things that others have done to give him moments of pleasure, for example, coffee. Fox will think about all the people involved who allow him to enjoy his coffee in the morning, from the farmers that picked the beans, to the people who roast, pack, and ship it. Putting your mind to think about the efforts needed to enjoy the simple pleasures you experience each day, can make you more appreciative, humble and grateful. (Foxx 2016)

The sustained happiness we get from gratitude has been studied. In a 2012 study, participants were asked to write a letter of thanks to someone who had been kind to them (identical to the exercise I was asked to do). The results showed participants who engaged in letter-writing reported an increase in happiness lasting for at least a month (Toepfer, Cichy and Peters 2012).

Gratitude has also been found to foster resilience. Resilience is defined as the ability to recover from or adjust to misfortune or change. Most of us in our lives are confronted with setbacks. Setbacks make life unpredictable and stressful and it is those moments between triumph and tragedy that builds character.

The brain is wired to bounce back from difficulties through experience and practice of habits which create the coping mechanisms that build resilience. Gratitude based habits focus your brain on positive triggers in the nervous system and, according to researchers at the University of California Davis, results in a 23% decrease in the stress hormone cortisol (UC Davis Health 2015).

An interesting study published in 2014 found another benefit of practicing gratitude: an increase in self-control. Researchers at Harvard found gratitude served as a tool for reducing impatience. Participants in the study showed higher self-control when they focused thoughts on life events they identified as being grateful for, as opposed to those they were happy or neutral about. Professor Ye Li comment on the potential of using gratitude as a tool for self-control stating:

"Showing that emotion can foster self-control and discover a way to reduce impatience with simple gratitude exercises opens up tremendous possibilities for reducing a wide range of societal ills from impulse buying and insufficient saving to obesity and smoking.

Bra*in*sights

The current findings argue strongly for a second route to combat excessive impatience – a route that can operate relatively intuitively and thus effortlessly from the bottom up." (DeSteno, et al. 2014)

By practicing gratitude, it is possible to increase self-control without a demanding behavior modification program based on willpower, which plenty of studies confirm seldom work.

The goal should be for you to make gratitude a habit. To move being grateful over to an automated process that is effortlessly triggered. Your brain continuously creates new neural pathways, making connections between two ideas, or objects, and sending electronic pulses between corresponding neurons. The more you use these neural connections the more efficient and automatic they become. The more you practice gratitude, the stronger the synaptic efficiency will become and the more self-control you will have.

Start by giving thanks for another day from the moment you wake and look for ways you can express thanks for those around you who have made your life easier, more rewarding, more interesting or enjoyable. Tell them what they have done for you, send them an email, text message, a Facebook IM, and let them know. End the day by taking a few moments to reflect on what you have and what you can give thanks for. Write it in a journal, use a mobile app to save it, or write it on a Post-It note and stick it to your computer screen, or mirror where you will see it at the start of the next day.

I have tried in my life to show gratitude for the things people do for me. I have thanked often individual customers for their business and continued support and for opening the door to their company to what I offer. The reaction has been often some embarrassment, but I know they appreciate it. It takes only a moment, and it has far-reaching benefits for you and for them.

In my business producing insulin pump cases for children, radrr (radrr.com), I have created friendships with the people in China helping me to produce my products. I try to get to know them as people by asking them about their lives, their children, hobbies, where they have traveled and what their aspirations are.

Does it take more time? Yes, it does. But I have seen the results of my gratitude. I can hear in their voices the appreciation for my interest in them, and I see in my business they will do more to help me succeed, including faster service and more attention to detail. The gratitude I have extended to them is paid back.

This is what a good life is about and what we should aspire to every day: expressing our gratitude to others for being in our lives. There is a saying, "Your mind is a garden, your thoughts are the seeds. You can grow flowers, or you can grow weeds." Make a habit of planting more 'flowers' by using gratitude.

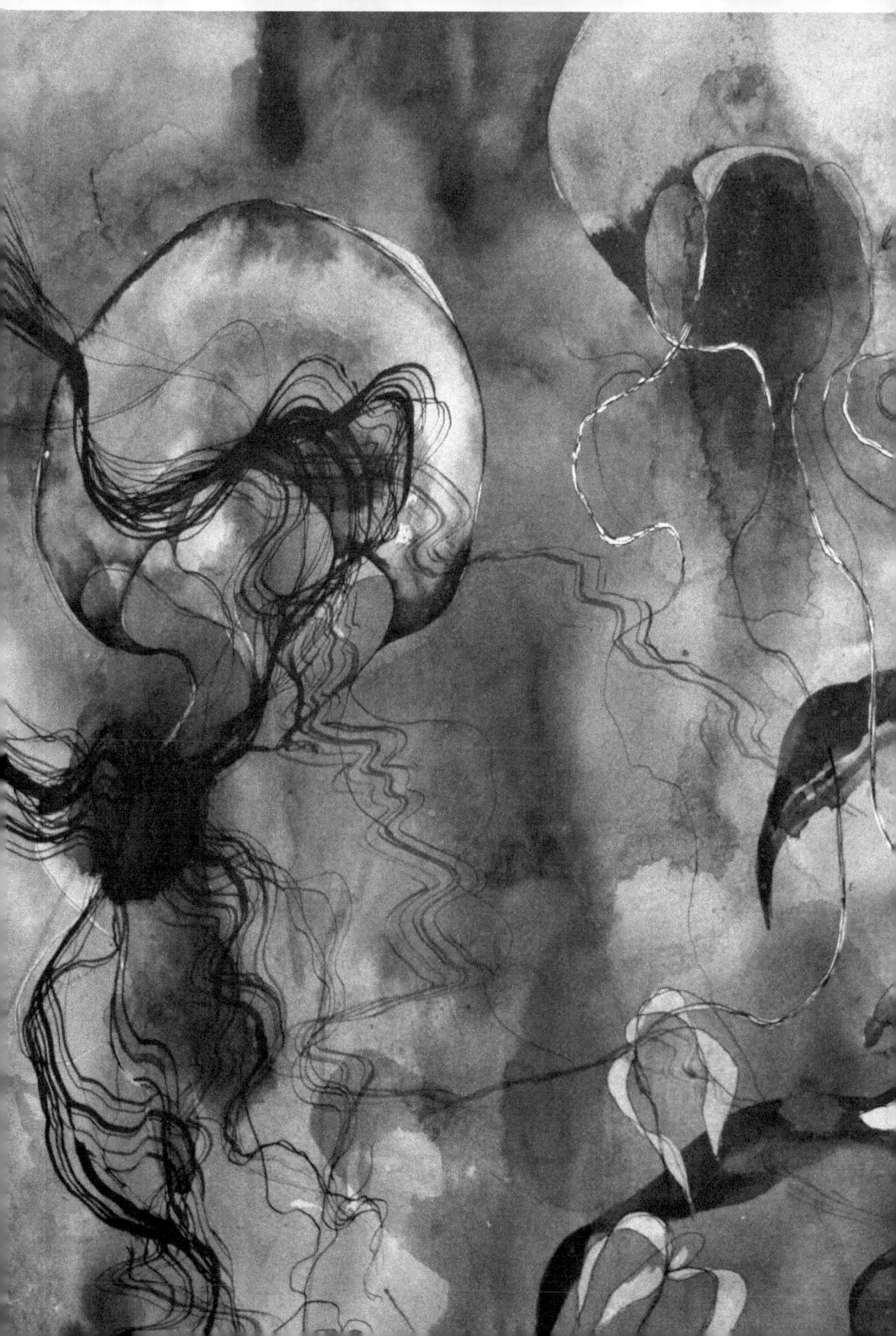

David C Winegar

YOUR BRAIN IS PLASTIC

Every man can, if he so desires, become the sculptor of his own brain.

Santiago Ramon y Cajal

As recently as the 1960s, most scientists believed growth in the brain could only occur in children and young adults. It was believed the brain stopped growing and its structure was set once we reached adulthood.

This view was still quite widely held when I was a young adult in the early 80s. There was a big push on in the US to prevent alcohol and drug abuse among young people and there were countless campaigns highlighting the ill effects of alcohol on the brain, proclaiming it kills brain cells and that you will never get those cells back.

Believing that I might be killing my brain off with a few drinks was a frightening thought, but this was not based on reliable science and it has since proven to be a myth. Moderate alcohol intake does not kill brain cells, or even damage them. Heavy excessive drinking can damage dendrites responsible for passing messages from one neuron to another, but your brain cells are not being killed (Mulholland, et al. 2018). Even dendrite damage can be reversed with therapy and training.

You probably know people, or have heard of, who have experienced debilitating strokes and have recovered through therapy. A meta-analysis of 13 fMRI studies of stroke victims with impaired motor function, provides evidence that the brain can recover function with targeted rehabilitation therapy (Lorie G. Richards 2008). The study looked at persons who had experienced motor function loss due to stroke, such as a decrease in the use of a hand or arm. It found overwhelming evidence to support programs of focused therapy as helpful in reactivating the damaged area of the brain and resulting in a higher possibility of recovery.

What we now know is that the brain can be 'taught' to work in other ways – to work around a damaged area and create new neural connections – a process called neurogenesis – to compensate for or overcome the damage. And if the brain can create new neural connections in times of distress, the hope is it can also create them in other instances.

But let's take one step back and look at the birth of neuroscience and what it can tell us about brain plasticity and neurogenesis.

Our first understandings of the brain

One of the most famous brain injury cases, and what many consider to be the birth of neuroscience, is the case of Phineas Gage. The story of his brain injury is thought to be the first documented case of a person with a severe brain injury surviving and being able to function and carry on with his life.

Source: Warren Anatomical Museum, Harvard Medical School.

In 1848, 25-year-old Gage was working as an explosives expert on the railroad in Cavendish, Vermont. On September 13, 1848, he was using a big tapping iron rod (43 inches long, 1,25 inches in diameter and weighing 13 pounds) to pack explosive powder into a hole to blow up a section of rock. Gage had done this countless time, but this time he skipped the critical step of covering the explosives with sand before tapping. The powder ignited and propelled the iron rod up penetrating the left side of his face and exiting through his skull.

It was a horrific accident, but Gage survived. In some reports it was reported that he didn't even lose consciousness and was alert enough to say to a doctor, "Here is business enough for you." All joking aside, Gage provided many years of study on the impact of the injury on his life, much

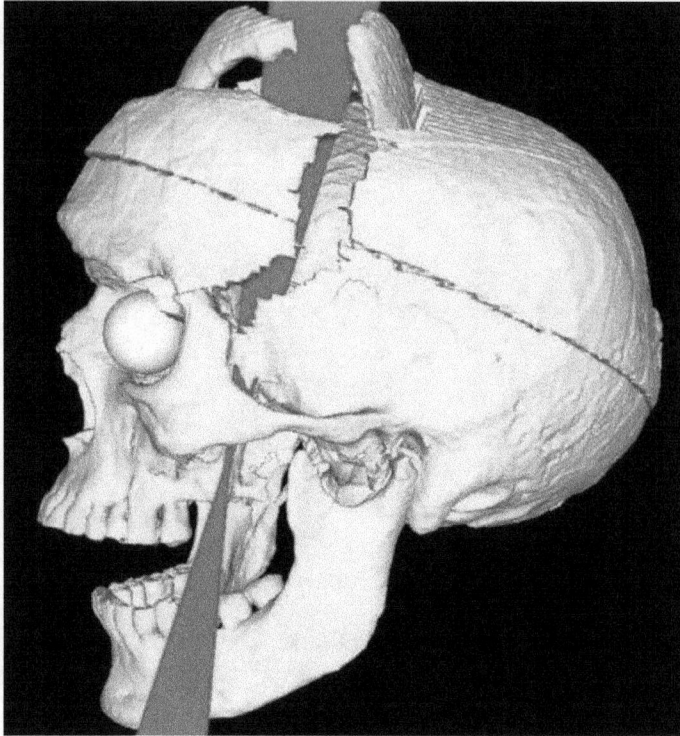

Source: By Van Horn JD, Irimia A, Torgerson CM, Chambers MC, Kikinis R, et al. Mapping Connectivity Damage in the Case of Phineas Gage.

of it carried out by Harvard Medical School doctor Henry Jacob Bigelow. Bigelow presented the first account of the observed changes in Gage's behavior following the accident:

"Previous to his injury, although untrained in the schools, he possessed a well-balanced mind, and was looked upon by those who knew him as a shrewd, smart businessman, very energetic and persistent in executing all his plans of operation. He could no longer stick to plans, shouted out the most offensive profanity, and showed little concern for those he worked with. He would make plans but fail to carry them out and that many of his friends described his personality as greatly changed, to the point that they felt he was no longer Gage." (Harlow 1850)

Gage's case had a tremendous influence on early neurology. Gage's damage to his prefrontal cortex (both right and left lobes) and the perceived changes to his personality gave rise to the idea of localization of brain function, or the idea that specific areas of our brain are responsible for individual functions.

Today, neuroscientists know much more about the role the prefrontal cortex plays in higher-order functions such as language, reasoning, and social processing.

There is much debate about his recovery and the validity of the reports on his personality changes. Much of the conjecture about his condition by doctors came not from first-hand observation but from secondary accounts, many of them years after his death. For those that knew Gage later in life they described a man who was fully functional and able to work well and hold down a demanding job requiring social interactions. After the accident he worked as a stagecoach driver in Chile for 7 years and reports from people that observed him in that job did not describe a person unable to function or socialize. This is where history and modern research intersect.

Gage's case is historically given as an example of brain injury and how it results in unrecoverable change, but the later accounts of Gage's life show he could function well and may have recovered completely from his injuries. Could Gage be one of the first cases of documented neurogenesis? Was his brain able to create new neural connections that allowed him to recover from his injuries and lead a normal life? It is not likely that we will ever know for certain, but as neuroscience provides more evidence supporting neurogenesis, it may be future interpretations of Gage's case will change.

The history of neurogenesis

It has been a long (and rocky) road to the acceptance of adult regeneration of neurons, or neurogenesis. The original discovery was made in 1965 by MIT professors Joseph Altman and Gopal Dar, in a study of rats (Das and Joseph 1965), but their findings were rejected by the established scientific community and the funding for continuing the work lost.

It would take nearly two and a half decades before the idea of neurogenesis was successfully revived by esteemed Rockefeller University neuroscientist Fernando Nottebohm. Studying adult canaries, he discovered their brains do create new nerve cells in adulthood, replacing older cells (Nottebohm 1989).

The debate on the existence of neurogenesis in adults is still alive with a study published in March of 2018 undertook by Nottebohm's former protégé who concluded that neurogenesis ends in childhood. (Sorrells, et al. n.d.) But there is much debate over how the research was conducted and if the methods used were able to detect new neural formation. Gerd Kempermann, a neuroscientist at the Technical University of Dresden explains:

"Just because the scientists don't see new neurons doesn't mean they aren't there. Alvarez-Buylla and his colleagues used marker molecules to tag immature in brain samples that had been collected and prepared for analysis within 48 hours after an individual died. Whether these markers can reliably tag young neurons depends a lot on the quality of the tissue, which is influenced by how soon after death the samples are treated to keep them from decaying." (Guglielmi 2018)

In April of 2018 a study published in the journal *Cell Stem Cell* countered, saying that it was possible:

"[H]ealthy older subjects without cognitive impairment, neuropsychiatric disease, or treatment display preserved neurogenesis. It is possible that ongoing hippocampal neurogenesis sustains human-specific cognitive function throughout life and that declines may be linked to compromised cognitive-emotional resilience." (Boldrini, et al. 2018)

One of the difficulties in researching the human brain and neurogenesis is it is not currently possible to do on living subjects. All the research done so far has been postmortem and has focused on identifying markers that suggest new neural growth rather than actual new neural growth. At the moment, no technology exists for viewing the creation of new neural in a person no longer alive. The debate is likely to continue until new brain imaging tools that can view new neurons in a live person's brain is created.

Why does it matter if we can generate new neurons or not? The idea that humans can create new neurons is something that provides hope for everything from the treatment of depression, to the treatment of age-associated cognitive decline and opens the door to expanding the capabilities of the human brain. Neurogenesis, if it exists or can be created in adults, represents a new frontier of possibilities for mankind.

One of the scientists at the forefront of the study of neurogenesis is Sandrine Thuret of King's College London. Her lab has been involved in multiple research projects in recent years supporting neurogenesis.

Her research has looked both at the brains of mice and humans, and in each she found evidence of neurogenesis in the hippocampus (the area responsible for long-term and spatial memory and mood regulation). In fact, the human adult brain is producing around 700 new neurons each day and by the time we reach 50 years of age, we have replaced all the neurons we developed as children with our adult produced ones (Kirsty L. Spalding 2013). In another study published in April of 2018 reported that healthy people in their 70s have just as many young neurons as do teenagers and young adults (Boldrini, et al. 2018).

New neurons are important for learning. They have found in the lab that if the outer brain is blocked from producing new neurons in the hippocampus, it directly affects learning, especially spatial recognition (TEDTalks 2015).

In a study done on rats at the University of Gothenburg in 1998 researchers found that adult rats housed in an enriched environment, one including climbing ladders, platforms, paper, nesting materials, cardboard nests, and new toys every three or four days, had an increased rate of neurogenesis and had an improved performance in spatial learning tasks (Nilsson M 1999). The research confirmed not only the formation of new neurons but also environment plays a role in connections surviving and, perhaps more importantly, an increase in performance. Think of the implications for society if we can carry this research over to humans.

Side note: You might wonder what can rat brain research teach us about humans. Let's take a moment and address the question of why rats are good subjects for researching the human brain. According to Andrea Chiba, a University of California at San Diego professor and cognitive scientist, "rats are a good model for humans because a lot of the structure and connectivity that exists in human brains also exists in rats. Rodents are genetically like humans and have short life spans which helps to study them over generations." (Chiba 2015)

The Gothenburg study has not been duplicated on humans and there is a lot of difficulty involved in carrying out such research on human subjects. But the promise shown has far-reaching implications for how we treat everything from brain injuries and stroke, to degenerative diseases such as Alzheimer's. The ability to stimulate new neural growth and then activate them to remain in place, would be an important leap forward for humankind.

Proof of plasticity

One of the most cited research publications on brain plasticity is one carried out by the University College London. Neuroscientist Eleanor Maguire had been interested in the memories of animals, especially those who had highly formed memories. Some birds and mammals cache their food and, contrary to popular belief, they use their memory and not their noses to find their hiding spots. The study of those animal's brains revealed a much larger hippocampus, the area of the brain responsible for memory and spatial navigation. Maguire wondered if humans involved in complicated spatial memory tasks also had larger hippocampi.

Being a Londoner, Maguire was well acquainted with the difficulty London cab drivers have in passing the infamous taxi drivers license simply known as 'The Knowledge.' The test requires drivers to memorize more than 25 000 streets and thousands of landmarks. It takes between three and four years of study and an average of 12 attempts to pass the exam.

Maguire followed a group of 79 trainee taxi drivers taking fMRI snapshots of their brain structures and studied their performance on memory tasks. The initial scans and cognitive performance tests showed a high degree of similarity in all 79 peoples' hippocampi in regard to size, performance on working memory, and long-term memory (Eleanor A. Maguire 2000).

A follow-up four years later found 39 of the original 79 had passed the test and obtained their licenses. Re-testing the participants Maguire found those who passed performed far better on the memory tests and the size of their hippocampi were considerably larger. In fact, the longer the person had been driving a taxi in London, the larger their hippocampus (Eleanor A. Maguire 2000).

The study provides some proof that the brain can reorganize itself when it is exposed to learning and experience. The process it takes to get a London black cab taxi license is very demanding. Once a cabby gets the license, they are continually forced to update their knowledge, constantly rewiring their brains and creating new neural pathways. Every new customer that gets in their cab may require them to access 'The Knowledge' and apply it in a new way.

Maguire's work is important in demonstrating the brain can and does grow and change in adulthood and can even alter its physical structure based on new experience. The increase in spatial memory through nothing more than cognitive effort is a turning point in the understanding of the brain. If it is possible through focused and constant effort to reshape and rewire the brain to accommodate the need for additional abilities, it also points to the possibility to alter our brains for other functions.

Children can learn at phenomenal rates, taking in information and formulating new neural connections at an astonishing rate. It is theorized that the reason for this ability is because the brain is a blank slate.

That the brain is a blank slate, or a tabula rasa, has been around for over a thousand years, but it is mostly associated in modern times with English philosopher John Locke who developed a theory of knowledge as a collection of sensory experiences. Locke writes in *An Essay Concerning Human Understanding*, published in 1690:

"Let us then suppose the mind to be, as we say, white paper void of all characters, without any ideas; how comes it to be furnished? Whence comes it by that vast store, which the busy and boundless fancy of man has painted on it, with an almost endless variety? Whence has it all the materials of reason and knowledge? To this I answer, in one word, from experience: in that, all our knowledge is founded; and from that it ultimately derives itself." (Locke 1998)

Locke was perceptive in his idea that experience writes the words to the blank paper of the child's mind. Every new experience causes the brain to form synapses at a rapid rate, and faster than at any other time of life, as the brain tries to fill the blank slate with the information it needs to thrive in the world. It is a fact that children learn faster than adults because of their ability to rapidly make new connections.

To optimize the growth of a child's brain it is important to expand the number of experiences and the exposure to new ideas. It is this exposure to many experiences which builds what we could describe as wisdom. One reason teenagers make risky and poor decisions, is because their brains are not yet developed and lack wisdom.

One study conducted by the National Institute of Mental Health found that teenagers can show 'remarkable control' sometimes, even greater impulse control than adults. Put emotion into the equation and it is a different story. Teenagers, particularly males, are influenced negatively by emotion and performance falters. The diminished ability to make good decisions in the 'heat of the moment,' when critical decisions need to be made, is difficult for teens. (Casey and Caudle 2013)

One theme of this book has been in connecting behavior to the evolution of the brain, which can also be done with the development of children's brains. From an evolutionary perspective it was important for children to rapidly learn as a mechanism for survival within the social group. Learning the language of the group, adapting to the social norms, and being able to quickly comprehend how to fit into the group was important to success. The faster you can adapt and learn the norms of the group, the higher the probability of survival.

It was also important to be less cautious and more tolerable of risk as a teenager. Teenagers need to break out of the protective circle of their parents and set out on their own to find their place as adults in society. Without a lower threshold to risk, they could not do this. Taking risks and learning from them is an essential part of becoming a useful member of society. It is no different today. Teens need to go through this process to build their wisdom to make better decisions as adults.

Watching children learn in their early years is a humbling experience. I was fortunate in my mid-20s to get a job as an international teacher at a school in Helsinki, Finland. This school was established in 1946 by a group of Catholic nuns from St. Louis, Missouri, with the mission to teach Finnish children English. Students started school in August at five, and even if they didn't speak a word of English when they started, by December of that year they were fluent. The rate they could pick up the language was remarkable, a testament to the ease of learning a second language at an early age.

My son, who is now 16, was also exposed to two languages from day one of his birth. My wife spoke her native Finnish and I spoke my native English to him. We tried as parents to be consistent in not mixing the languages. I had noticed from my teaching days that when students started at a later age, around the age of 8, it became much more difficult for them to compartmentalize the languages. I recall one student from Poland who started at the school when he was 7 and struggled with not having any 'mother tongue.' He spoke English at school, Polish at home, and Finnish with his friends. The environment put a heavy strain on his brain's ability to express his thoughts in any one language. My son can easily change his language based on who he wanted to talk to. He has two mother tongues.

Research has connected language learning to enhanced brain plasticity. In a paper published in the Journal of Scientific Reports, researchers from the Higher School of Economics (HSE), in Moscow, Russia, and the University of Helsinki, in Finland, found that early language learning plays a significant role in the rapid formation of memory circuits for coding new information. EEG studies of participants in the study found that the brain reacted faster with the acquisition of more languages. (Lilli Kimppa 2016)

Although this research only looks at the acquisition and uptake of new words in languages, it is not too much of a leap of faith to believe learning of languages also helps in the rapid update of other information by the brain. As the brain learns to adapt to faster processing of information as caused by the learning of language, is there any reason the same brain mechanisms will not carry over to other forms of information? It will be interesting to follow the subsequent research into this area.

The brain's plasticity is not limited to language or mapping, it reshapes, or rewires, itself based on exposure to new experience and stimuli. If we take the simple task of walking, we can see our brains at work creating connections. Walking on a street in your neighborhood that has just undergone new construction triggers the brain to form new connections. You would not have to think too much, if all, about walking on this street as it is something you have done 100s of times each year, but now being under construction, the surface has changed, and your brain must go to work. Each step you take on the unfamiliar new surface causes your brain to go into processing mode with the brain trying to make sense of the new stimuli. It attempts to match the input with what is stored and adjust your leg and foot movements to navigate better the new surface.

It is during this process where you are undergoing neurogenesis, creating new connections, and learning. We do the same each time we have a new experience. Each time we undergo learning of something new.

How to stimulate new brain connections

The surface of the earth is soft and impressible by the feet of men; and so with the paths which the mind travels. How worn and dusty, then, must be the highways of the world, how deep the ruts of tradition and conformity!

Henry David Thoreau

In a study published in 2017 by researchers at the University of Alabama at Birmingham, neuroscientists conducted research on adult mice using a state-of-the-art system to investigate the dentate gyrus of the hippocampus, the brain system responsible for the formation of new memories. They found that new neurons were forming – and, more interestingly, they found those new neurons were 'weaving' themselves into pre-existing connections, resulting in refined connections (Adlaf, et al. 2017).

For the first time, research has identified that the brain creates not only new connections, but the new connections can alter existing connections to change old memories. It means humans have the possibility to move away from the existing ways of doing, what Thoreau described as the deep ruts of conformity, and create modifications of those 'deep ruts.' The potential exists to put aside past events that have caused us trauma, anxiety, and stress and replace them with versions less painful. It is possible to change our brains by pruning the patterns and connections holding us back from living our lives to the fullest.

The brains need to remove connections

The brain in infancy is prolific producing an abundance of new neural connections which become our stored memories. The brain produces an abundance of neural connections, far more than is needed. But the brain has limits to its ability to sustain connections. It prunes, or cuts off, connections it deems as unnecessary to make room for those it believes essential. "The process of pruning allows the brain to fine-tune its neural network and strengthen the connections between neurons important for brain function" (Ring 2016). Just as a gardener carefully prunes a bonsai tree to shape it and help it become stronger, your brain carefully trims connections to reinforce the important ones.

Remember our discussion on how your brain looks to conserve energy? You might wonder why your brain would spend energy creating far more connections than needed? Researchers believe the reason is flexibility. The more connections created, the more flexible your brain can be. Danielle Bassett, a researcher at the University of Pennsylvania, has looked at how the brain operates when it is learning and has determined that brains with a high degree of flexibility learn best (Bassett, et al. 2011).

What Bassett's team did was to put volunteers into fMRI scanners and then taught them something new. As they learned, the neuroscientist watched as the neural networks rewired themselves. This research was one of the first to show in action the connections being created on the fly and illustrated that even in simple learning, the brain is creating a complex weave of connections between many regions. Those with a higher flexibility appeared to learn faster. (Bassett, et al. 2011)

It was once believed neural pruning ended shortly after birth, but as with neurogenesis this view has changed. In 1979, Peter Huttenlocher of the University of Chicago showed that excess neural production and pruning continues long after birth. Using an electron microscope, he examined the autopsied brains of deceased humans and discovered that the synapses, the tiny connections between neurons, decreased rapidly during adolescence. The brain in adolescence appears to go into a period where it aggressively prunes redundant connections to streamline your brain. (Feinberg 2017)

Pruning of excess connections helps to explain why people have trouble recovering from a brain injury. We do not have redundant systems able to take over when we lose a connection due to injury (Feinberg 2017). It can also explain why many major mental illnesses emerge in adolescence, the theory being that the brain prunes the wrong connections (Feinberg 2017) (Zagorski 2016).

Breaking habits by pruning connections

Habits are patterns embedded in our brains difficult to give up. Those patterns can only be changed if we prune the connections and replace them with new ones, 'unlearning' the bad habits. Habits are not a single isolated event, but the culmination of a series of events linked together in a sequential chain (Amaya and Smith 2018).

For example, my morning routine is very much a habit defined by a series of small movements. I get out of bed, I put my slippers on and my watch, go to the bathroom, and head to the coffee machine. I turn it on, grind the coffee beans, fill the espresso filter, wait for the water to heat, take a cup and turn on the hot water, run the cup under the hot water for a minute, then place it under the machine and make my coffee. This is just the first 10 minutes of my habitual morning routine, a cascade of small movements arranged into a chunk of automated behavior that is a habit.

We have many habits, like making coffee in the morning, that are innocent and even necessary to our daily survival and well-being. But there are also many habits we have formed that are not good for us and detrimental to our well-being.

According to researcher Ann Graybiel from the Massachusetts Institute of Technology, in a 2016 study published in the *Journal of Neurophysiology,* when a signaling habit has taken shape, breaking it becomes a difficult endeavor. She describes the habit as structured with a distinct 'high-level' beginning signal initiating it and a distinct end signal that says it has been completed (Kyle S. Smithc 2016). Along the chain are rewards that keep us motivated to reach the end. To break a habit, one must interrupt the high-level signal trigger initiating it.

For many bad habits the trigger can be something simple and avoidable. Nora Volkow, head of the National Institute of Drug Abuse, found that images alone can increase the dopamine in our brains and give us the urge to indulge in a bad habit. That could look like a heroin addict seeing someone they have used with, an overeater seeing an ad for a Big Mac, or a smartphone addict seeing the pop-up notification (Goldstein 2018).

The only way to break the habit is to make ourselves aware of the trigger, and then modify our behavior to break that trigger, to prune the connection from our minds.

One thing that must be right before you start the process of breaking a habit, is the environment. If you don't have the right environment, where your brain can work to create new neural connections, it will be even harder to break the habit. Remember the rat experiment where the ones with the enhanced environment could create more neural connections?

One reason people addicted to drugs and alcohol go to treatment centers and isolate themselves from the past is to create an environment that promotes change by removing themselves from the people and places that served as triggers to their addiction. This is not only true of drug-induced habits, but also bad work habits. Changing the environment should be your priority. What can you change that will make the environment more supportive of your new habit?

For example, if you have a bad habit of procrastinating in the morning and getting overly distracted, you could change your physical position at work. Interrupting the chain of how you work, will put a focus on the need to change. Try moving your computer or desk, even sitting at a different angle, or standing, can all have a positive impact on helping you to get your brain off the train track that is sending you towards that bad habit.

Repetition and consistent practice are needed to embed the pattern to our brains, and it takes longer than we think to establish a new habit. In a study conducted by Phillippa Lally at the University College London, 96 volunteers were asked to create a new habit and carry it out daily. The habit needed to be an eating, drinking, or activity-based behavior. For example, drink a bottle of water with breakfast.

Findings showed that it took between 18 and 254 days for the behavior to become a habit. The time it took differed based on the behavior, circumstances, and the person, but what is important to know is that it takes a considerable amount of time. The average was 66 days, or 2 months of constant practice before a behavior becomes automatic (Lally, et al. 2010). To create a new habit takes consistent repetition and a high degree of self-control.

Most of you can see the difficulties in establishing a new habit. How many of you have made New Year's resolutions promising to undertake a plan to improve yourself? Statistics show that 92% of us do not follow through with our resolutions. We are not able to stay motivated enough to make it through the minimum of 66 days we need to make that simple habit stick, like drinking more water, we are even worse at the longer-term goals of getting fit.

If you try something new, and it doesn't stick as a habit in a couple of weeks, don't feel discouraged. Find comfort in the fact that it is supposed to take longer. Stick at it and find the intrinsic motivation to keep yourself going through the tough times. Find a partner that shares the same goal and enlist them to help you. Support from others is a great motivator and can be the extra push needed to keep you on track when we want to give up.

Time to get in the game

One of the bad habits your brain has in undertaking new things is the habit it has of equating being at the game with being in the game. Let me explain. Let's say you follow a specific team or individual, and you get to see a sporting event where they're playing. For me one of the earliest sporting matches I got excited about was the Wimbledon tennis final of Borg vs. McEnroe played on US Independence Day, the 4th of July, in 1981.

Having played tennis for a couple of years, I loved the game and the duel between Borg and McEnroe was thrilling to watch. My mirror neurons put me in McEnroe's shoes and I could imagine myself on the courts of the All England Lawn and Tennis and Croquet Club.

This is what the brain likes to do. It puts us in the place of the athletes on the field. Just as a good movie puts you in the shoes of the characters, in a good sporting event you imagine yourself in the shoes of the athletes. When the one we are supporting scores or wins, our brains process it as though we have scored or won. We get a similar chemical high just from watching.

This is all great fun when we are watching sporting matches, but the brain initiates the same reaction to many other things. Take, for example, that business leadership forum where you saw Barack Obama, Simon Sinek,

Deepak Chopra, or even actor Will Smith, you find yourself riveted by what speakers are telling you and agree 100% with their advice about how to be better. Your brain delivers a reward and tells you "OK, yeah I got it, this is fantastic, great insight and principles to live by." You are at the game, enjoying it and getting the brain rush the same as I got watching McEnroe beat Borg in the 1981 final. The problem is, that is where it ends.

Once your brain has transmitted the good feeling, given you the dopamine hit, it is job done for the brain. It makes you feel as if you have accomplished something just by sitting there and listening. The reward has come by being *at* the game and herein is the problem. Few of us take it the next step to get *in* the game and act to apply what we have just experienced.

Neuroscience has shown that anticipation can release dopamine and many scientists are now calling dopamine the anticipation molecule. The first study in humans that looked at the power of anticipation and the delivery of reward was done by Stanford University professor Brian Knutson published in 2008 in *NeuroReport*.

Knutson study gamblers and tracked blood flow in the brain via fMRI scans as they gambled. The pivotal finding was that the brain's pleasure center (the nucleus accumbens) was not stimulated when getting the reward (winning) but rather in anticipation of it. Knutson concluded that "what draws us to act is not the sensation we receive from the reward itself but the need to alleviate the craving for that reward." (Knutson, et al. 2008)

Anticipation alone will not release a large dose of dopamine, there must also be a realistic opportunity to receive the reward.

Let me give a business example from my work life I have an ongoing struggle with my brain about. One thing I must do in my coaching and training business is to sell. It involves contacting customers and trying to convince them to meet with me and discuss my services. My brain tries to keep me from getting in the game by delivering the reward for acting in incidental ways.

I will think of a customer I believe would be interested in my services and look up their website, and even take it a step further and head over to LinkedIn and identify people I should contact. I add them to my CRM system, and this is the point where my brain steps in and delivers a reward. The problem is I have yet to get in the game. I have not contacted anyone to let them know I exist or how my fantastic neuroscience-based programs can help them.

Getting in the game is difficult for the brain and one of the reasons the self-help business is such a big one. Your brain delivers the reward by doing little more than watching, listening, and reading. It pats us on the back and says, "Well done, you now know what to do." Never mind you have yet to do anything. The statistics show that few of us can push ourselves to get into the game.

Many of you who are reading this book will fall into this trap of not getting into the game. You have invested in this book by purchasing it, you spend the time to read, you likely find something interesting that could be applied to your life, but to get to the next step you have to struggle against your brain, which is telling you you've finished working, go and relax.

EPILOGUE

I began this book with the statement we are living at a remarkable time in history where the black box that is our brain is giving up its secrets. I have covered over 210 original research studies in this book, most of them published within the last three years. It's worth taking a few moments to reflect on the key themes of this book with a view to the future to inspire you to take the next step and put neuroscience to work for you to live, love, and lead an extraordinary life.

A key theme of Brainsights was the importance of chemicals (hormones) and their influence on behavior. Behavior is never random. Our brain chemicals have evolved to play a specific role in promoting survival over tens of thousands of years. It is wrong to say they cause behavior because they do not. But their influence works to lower the threshold of self-control by cutting off access to your S2 high-order processing. The result is emotional instead of thoughtful responses to stimuli leading to unproductive and sometimes self-destructive behavior. Emotionally driven responses are fast and were needed on the plains of Africa where speed was more important to survival than thoughtfully considered responses.

Your brain is always looking for fast, easy, and certain. It is lazy and for a good reason. It sees danger around every corner and is more likely to see risk than opportunity in every situation. To prepare for the apocalypse, it is convinced is coming, it looks for every available opportunity to shut down energy-intensive complex S2 thinking. It whispers in your subconscious, "Be vigilant and preserve your energy."

It is natural to fight with your lazy brain and its desire to bypass the process of self-control. To be more successful it is important to not fight against but work within the limitations of your evolved brain. The stress and pressure put on yourself to change results from engaging in actions that are, from a brain perspective, unwinnable. A better way is to find actions to distract, redirect, and reappraise your behavior rather than suppress it. These actions will always be easier for the brain and more likely to result in positive and beneficial outcomes. As neuroscientist Robert Sapolsky says:

"It's great if your frontal cortex lets you avoid temptation, allowing you to do the harder, better thing. But it's usually more effective if doing that better thing has become so automatic that it isn't hard. And it's often easiest to avoid temptation with distraction and reappraisal rather than willpower." (R. M. Sapolsky 2017)

The brain is socially wired. It looks for ways to increase its prosocial stance by directing your behavior to benefit the people in your close social group. The chemical oxytocin fuels and nourishes your social orientation. Being other-focused is about showing trust and working towards beneficial goals. It is also about showing empathy and understanding. When our brains are working to promote mutual benefits oxytocin locks us in sync with one another and helps us to be more caring and collaborative. But before you can get the benefits of oxytocin you need to actively engage in behaviors that promote its production. Showing you care and are as concerned with other's success and happiness as you are with your own, is the place to start. It requires being more aware of your own behaviors and directing them towards positive, prosocial, oxytocin releasing actions.

Brain plasticity, harnessing the power of the brain to create new neural connections and re-wire itself, offers terrific possibilities for the future. Neuroscience is unlocking the processes involved in creating new connections. Researchers have overturned the previously held belief that the brain stops 'growing' after adolescence, confirming the brain continues to generate new connections throughout our whole lives. It is up to you to embrace this plasticity of the brain and maximize your own ability to form new connections.

There are many documented cases of people who have been able to use plasticity to recover from debilitating brain injuries. Focused therapeutic attention has been shown to create new pathways in the brain restoring lost functionality. In times of extreme need, for example in cases of stroke, it has been shown that we can direct our brains to new ways of working using nothing more than focused effort. If the brain can be altered in times of need, it suggests there exists the opportunity to use focus attention to change your brain to expose other abilities.

It can be argued that there is the potential for any of us to become an Einstein, a Picasso, or a Mozart. It is only a matter of unlocking the full potential of our brains. There are incredible documented stories of people who have had traumatic brain injuries and gained amazing new abilities. Abilities that have made them the definition of genius.

In 1994 Tony Cicoria, an orthopedic surgeon from New York, was struck by lightning in the head. Soon after his recovery, he experienced an overwhelming desire to play piano, an instrument he had previously had just a few lessons on as a boy. He spent every extra moment at the piano teaching himself to play. But there was something else at work in his brain. His own original music kept playing in his head and he soon was playing and composing original works. Today he performs his own intricate piano compositions and has a second career as a musician. The lightning had unlocked the musical genius in his brain. (Sacks 2003)

One of the most incredible examples, of what is known as "acquired savant syndrome," is the case of Jason Padgett. In 2002 he was attacked in a bar in Tacoma, Washington, and suffered a severe concussion. When he awoke in his hospital bed his view of the world could only be described as overlaid with a layer of math. Before the accident he was a college dropout with no interest in mathematics. Today he can picture complex geometrical shapes and is learning to understand the mathematical equations that his mind is visualizing. (Lewis 2014)

Padgett is one of the few to have undergone an fMRI scan to document the changes in his brain. What the scans revealed was unusually high activity in the left hemisphere of his brain, an area known for mathematical skills. What was more interesting was when that area of his brain was stimulated with magnetic pulses, his enhanced math skills temporarily disappeared.

In other studies neuroscientists have found when neurons die, they release brain-signaling chemicals that can increase brain activity in surrounding areas. But often these changes fade after a short time. For Padgett, he was one of the rare cases where his injuries resulted in structural changes to his brain (Lewis 2014). These examples serve to prove there is hidden potential in your brain and it is possible to unlock them, hopefully in ways other than through severe injury.

Pharmaceutical and technology start-ups are all working on drugs and devices that can unlock the hidden abilities of our brains. Although it is beyond the scope of this book to go into too many specifics, it is worth briefly mentioning. There are more than 500 new medications in development for neurological disorders for everything from chronic pain, multiple sclerosis, Alzheimer's and brain tumors (America's Biopharmeceutical Companies 2018). One of the key focus areas is Alzheimer's as it is a condition that specifically impairs cognitive function. The US Food and Drug Administration has already approved several drugs including one that improves alertness, a key factor in cognitive performance (Mehlman 2004). These drugs are not only for the cognitively impaired, they have also shown promise for improving abilities in healthy people.

The military has been experimenting with drugs and electrical devices. A drug called Modafinil originally developed to treat people with narcolepsy, excessive sleepiness, has been studied by the military as an aid to sustain alertness and performance in aviators and has proven to be highly effective (Caldwell, et al. 2000). They have also recently been experimenting with electrical devices, known as transcranial direct current stimulation (tDCS), to deliver low levels of direct current into the dorsolateral prefrontal cortex (S2 brain). Initial studies published in 2016 provided evidence that tDCS can "augment and enhance multitasking capability in a human operator" (Nelson, et al. 2016).

Let's not forget that humankind has a long history of using cognitive performance-enhancing drugs. The main one being caffeine. Over 2.25 billion cups of coffee are consumed each day. A review of the data on the effects of caffeine on cognitive performance shows it enhances attention, vigilance, and reaction time when taken in doses equivalent to one to two cups of coffee (32-300 mg – 1 cup of coffee has 90-150 mg of caffeine) (Tom M.McLellana 2016). Enhancing the brain through drugs and devices is near and holds promise for a future where we can eliminate some of the barriers to unlocking the full potential of our brains.

We do not have to wait for artificial means to change our brains and enhance our lives. Much research has already shown that it is possible through focused attention. The London taxi cab research showed people can change the structure of their brains through nothing more than focused and repeat attention to a task. Brain scans of monks with thousands of hours of meditation experience also showed the possibility for altering the brain through focused attention, and even the ability to move complicated S2 brain processes over to automated S1 processes.

What does this mean for us mere mortals, those of us who don't have thousands of hours to invest? Other studies have shown you can change your brain by developing simple habits. Actions like expressing gratitude to others and a simple listing of those things you are thankful for, assists in directing thoughts to places of positivity. This positive outlook has a direct effect on reducing stress which brings a noticeable improvement in well-being. Even modest changes in your daily routine and habits can improve overall satisfaction with your life and help alleviate the brain's natural proclivity for pessimism.

What I hope this book has illustrated is the brain needs structure to change and change always starts by performing a single action. Too often it is thought to get a better outcome it is necessary to first change behavior, but behavior is a sum of your actions and takes longer. A single action, on the other hand, if done consistently, will lead to long-term behavior change.

Just today I read an excellent example of an action leading to significant life change. A connection of mine on LinkedIn shared the philosophy of author and sports figure Gabrielle Reece called 'going first' (Wee 2018). Going first is about directing your actions towards being the one to take a risk and make the first move. Be the first to say hello and start a conversation when someone makes eye contact with you or be the first to smile and acknowledge another.

Gabrielle reminds us that life is short and if we let opportunities pass us by because we wait for others to make the first move, we will live a life of regret. Everything can change in an instant. Every day you have once-in-a-lifetime experiences and when you take an "I'm going first" attitude you increase the possibility to maximize the positive side of those experiences. A quote from James Keller sums it up nicely: "A candle loses nothing by lighting another candle." Use going first to light the candle of another and you take the first small action towards an exceptional life.

Small actions leading to better experiences should be your goal. Experience is at the heart of human existence. It is what shapes our understanding of everything around us, what embeds our learning, and what forms what is held in memory. It cannot be stressed enough the role experience plays in the formation of your brain. Who you are is a sum of the experiences stored in your brain. You use those experiences to test new stimuli and make with breathtaking speed decisions on how to respond.

Expanding the number of experiences you have is an action to take to change your brain. Seek new experiences wherever and whenever you can. "Think different" as Steve Jobs so brilliantly reminded us. It should not be thought of as a clever marketing ploy but as a philosophy to live life by. It is through different thinking that the brain creates new pathways and connections. Each time the brain is forced to look at something new, it activates a web of connections that require new pathways. Doing this changes your brain and expands your database of experiences for future use. Write a book, learn to paint, play guitar, travel, learn a new language, make new friends, try a new job – experience life and your brain will thrive.

I want to close with one last thought. It is easy to read a book, watch a lecture, view a documentary, or talk to a friend and get countless ideas on how to make your life exceptional. Ideas are cheap and brain easy. However, if you do not put those ideas into action, take a step to make something new happen, create a catalyst to change your brain, those ideas will be pruned and left to die. To put neuroscience to work to change your life, you must get in the game. Don't sit on the sidelines and cheer at all the great ideas, take one, put your feet on the field, and take a step towards making something happen.

As the renowned neuroscientist Dr. Karl Pribram said in a lecture in 1987:

"The brain thwarts progress with old habits and imaginary evils and is maddeningly prone to waiting for the big miracle or easy solution that never comes, never realizing that one small change and then another could have won it all." (Cooper 2017)

Get inspired, take the new experiences from reading this book, make one small change, and you will be on the path to winning it all.

David C Winegar

ABOUT THE AUTHOR

David C Winegar is an author, trainer, coach, speaker, and applied neuroscience advocate who travels the world helping organizations and individuals to achieve more through a better understanding of human behavior. His work has taken him to four continents, coaching 1 000s of people from over 70 countries.

Before getting his MBA in organizational behavior and eBusiness from the University of Pittsburgh, he had a diverse work background including; working at the Smithsonian Institution's American History Museum, at the National Archives of the United States of America as a top-secret records declassification expert, and an international teacher of history and geography in Helsinki, Finland.

Since receiving his MBA in 1995, he has been in no less than six tech start-up companies, 3 in the US and 3 in Finland, including a forerunner to Twitter and one of the first mobile email services. For the last 11 years, he has been running his organizational development and coaching consulting firm, Absolute-North Ltd., which uses the latest psychological and neuroscience research to develop people. He has developed an experiential learning method called Artificial Experience Building, which uses neuroscience-backed research to commit learning to long-term memory better.

David's work has been in a broad spectrum of industries, everything from mobile gaming, and SAS companies, to industrial equipment, shipping, and machinery.

He lives in Helsinki, Finland, with his wife Satu, son Tomas, and his French Briard dog Leo.

David C Winegar

BIBLIOGRAPHY

Adlaf, Elena W, Ryan J. Vaden, Anastasia J Niver, Allison F Manuel, Vincent C. Onyilo, Matheus T Araujo, Cristina V. Dieni, et al. 2017. "Adult-born neurons modify excitatory synaptic transmission to existing neurons." *eLife* 6. Accessed 8 24, 2018. https://elifesciences.org/articles/19886.

Adrian M. Haith, Thomas R. Reppert, Reza Shadmehr. 2012. "Evidence for Hyperbolic Temporal Discounting of Reward in Control of Movements." *The Journal of Neuroscience* 32 (34): 11727-11736. Accessed 7 3, 2018. https://ncbi.nlm.nih.gov/pmc/articles/pmc3462010.

Alcaro, Antonio, Robert Huber, and Jaak Panksepp. 2007. "Behavioral Functions of the Mesolimbic Dopaminergic System: an Affective Neuroethological Perspective." *Brain Research Reviews* 56 (2): 283-321. Accessed 8 7, 2018. http://caspar.bgsu.edu/~lobsterman/page/papers/2007alchubpan.pdf.

Amabile, Teresa M., and Steven J. Kramer. 2011. "The Power of Small Wins." *Harvard Business Review*. Accessed 8 8, 2018. http://hbr.org/2011/05/the-power-of-small-wins/ar/1.

Amaya, Kenneth A, and Kyle S. Smith. 2018. "Neurobiology of habit formation." *Current opinion in behavioral sciences* 20: 145-152. Accessed 8 24, 2018. https://sciencedirect.com/science/article/pii/s235215461730089x.

America's Biopharmeceutical Companies. 2018. *Tackling Neurological Disorders in New Ways.* April 18. http://innovation.org/treatments/genomics/personalized-medicine/tackling-neurological-disorders-new-ways.

Amodio, David M. 2014. "The neuroscience of prejudice and stereotyping." *Nature Reviews Neuroscience* 15 (10): 670-682. Accessed 7 2, 2018. http://nature.com/articles/doi:10.1038/nrn3800.

Anderson, Scott, interview by Jesse Lawler. 2017. *The "Gut-Brain Axis" with Scott Anderson* (January 6).

Arif A Hamid, Jeffrey R Pettibone, Omar S Mabrouk, Vaughn L Hetrick, Robert Schmidt, Caitlin M Vander Weele, Robert T Kennedy, Brandon J Aragona & Joshua D Berke. 2015. "Mesolimbic dopamine signals the value of work." *Nature Neuroscience* 117-126.

Arnsten, Amy F.T. 2009. "Stress signalling pathways that impair prefrontal cortex structure and function." *Nature Reviews Neuroscience* 10 (6): 410-422. Accessed 8 20, 2018. https://ncbi.nlm.nih.gov/pmc/articles/pmc2907136.

Bra*in*sights

Athalye, Vivek R., Fernando J. Santos, Jose M. Carmena, and Rui M. Costa. 2018. "Evidence for a neural law of effect." *Science* 359 (6379): 1024-1029. Accessed 6 25, 2018. http://science.sciencemag.org/content/359/6379/1024.

Badt, Karin. 2013. *Mirror Neurons and Why We Love Cinema: A Conversation with Vittorio Gallese and Michele Guerra in Parma.* May 10. https://www.huffingtonpost.com/karin-badt/mirror-neurons-and-why-we_b_3239534.html.

Barrett, Lisa Feldman. 2017. "The theory of constructed emotion: an active inference account of interoception and categorization." *Social Cognitive and Affective Neuroscience* 12 (1): 1-23.

Barrett, Lisa Feldman. 2017. *You aren't at the mercy of your emotions – your brain creates them.* TED. December. https://www.ted.com/talks/lisa_feldman_barrett_you_aren_t_at_the_mercy_o f_your_emotions_your_brain_creates_them?utm_campaign=tedspread&utm_medium=referral&utm_source=tedcomshare&utm_sq=fu1izce2dp.

Bassett, D. S., N. F. Wymbs, M. A. Porter, P. J. Mucha, J. M. Carlson, and S. T. Grafton. 2011. "Dynamic reconfiguration of human brain networks during learning." *Proceedings of the National Academy of Sciences* 108 (18): 7641-7646. Accessed 11 23, 2018.

Baumeister, Roy E, Ellen Bratslavsky, Mark Muraven, and Dianne M. Tice. 1998. "Ego depletion : Is the active self a limited resource ?" *Journal of Personality and Social Psychology* 74 (5). Accessed 10 26, 2018. https://psychologytoday.com/files/attachments/584/baumeisteretal1998.pdf .

Benjamin C. Ampel, Mark Muraven and Ewan C. McNay. 2018. "Mental Work Requires Physical Energy: Self-Control Is Neither Exception nor Exceptional." *Frontiers in Psychology.*

Berker, Archy O. de, Robb B. Rutledge, Christoph Mathys, Louise Marshall, Gemma F. Cross, Raymond J. Dolan, and Sven Bestmann. 2016. "Computations of uncertainty mediate acute stress responses in humans." *Nature Communications* 7: 10996. Accessed 8 30, 2018. https://nature.com/articles/ncomms10996.

Berkman, Elliot T., and Emily B. Falk. 2013. "Beyond Brain Mapping Using Neural Measures to Predict Real-World Outcomes." *Current Directions in Psychological Science* 22 (1): 45-50. Accessed 7 3, 2018. https://ncbi.nlm.nih.gov/pmc/articles/pmc3903296.

Berkman, Elliot T., and Jordan S. Miller-Ziegler. 2013. "Imaging depletion: fMRI provides new insights into the processes underlying ego depletion*." *Social Cognitive and Affective Neuroscience* 8 (4): 359-361. Accessed 7 3, 2018. https://ncbi.nlm.nih.gov/pmc/articles/pmc3624962.

Boldrini, Maura, Camille Fulmore, Alexandria Tartt, Laika R. Simeon, Ina P. Pavlova, Verica Poposka, Gorazd Rosoklija, et al. 2018. "Human Hippocampal Neurogenesis Persists throughout Aging." *Cell Stem Cell* 22 (4). Accessed 8 23, 2018. http://cell.com/cell-stem-cell/fulltext/s1934-5909(18)30121-8.

Bos, Peter A., Peter A. Bos, Dennis Hofman, Erno J. Hermans, Erno J. Hermans, Estrella R. Montoya, Simon Baron-Cohen, Jack van Honk, and Jack van Honk. 2016. "Testosterone reduces functional connectivity during the 'Reading the Mind in the Eyes' Test." *Psychoneuroendocrinology* 68: 194-201. Accessed 11 12, 2018. https://sciencedirect.com/science/article/pii/s0306453016300671.

Breckel TP, Thiel CM, Bullmore ET, Zalesky A, Patel AX, Giessing C. 2013 Sep 9;8(9):e74125. "Long-Term Effects of Attentional Performance on Functional Brain Network Topology." *PLoS One.*

Breuning, Loretta. 2012. *Breuning Books on the Mammal Brain.* https://innermammalinstitute.org/home-2/.

Broadbent, D. 1971. *Decision and Stress.* London: Academic.

Bucci, Rachel. 2018. "Sometimes When We Touch." *BrainWorld.* August 11. https://brainworldmagazine.com/sometimes-when-we-touch/.

Cahill, L., Gorski, L., & Le, K. 2003. "Enhanced Human Memory Consolidation With Post-Learning Stress: Interaction With the Degree of Arousal at Encoding." *Learning & Memory* (10): 270-274.

Caldwell, John A., J. Lyn Caldwell, Nicholas K. Smyth, and Kecia K. Hall. 2000. "A double-blind, placebo-controlled investigation of the efficacy of modafinil for sustaining the alertness and performance of aviators: a helicopter simulator study." *Psychopharmacology* 150 (3): 272-282. Accessed 11 29, 2018. https://link.springer.com/article/10.1007/s002130000450.

Carbon, Claus-Christian. 2014. "Understanding human perception by human-made illusions." *Frontiers in Human Neuroscience* 8: 566-566. Accessed 8 20, 2018. https://ncbi.nlm.nih.gov/pmc/articles/pmc4116780.

Carleton University. 2017. *Carleton Study Finds People Spending a Third of Job Time on Email.* April 20. https://newsroom.carleton.ca/archives/2017/04/20/carleton-study-finds-people-spending-third-job-time-email/.

Bra*in*sights

Carsten K. W. De Dreu, Lindred L.Greer, Gerben A. Van Kleef, Shaul Shalvi, Michel J. J. Handgraaf. 2011. "Oxytocin promotes human ethnocentrism." *Proceedings of the National Academy of Sciences of the United States of America* 108 (4). Accessed 7 30, 2018. http://pnas.org/content/108/4/1262.short.

Casey, B.J., and Kristina Caudle. 2013. "The Teenage Brain Self Control." *Current Directions in Psychological Science* 22 (2): 82–87. Accessed 11 23, 2018. https://ncbi.nlm.nih.gov/pmc/articles/pmc4182916.

Casey, B.J., Leah H. Somerville, Ian H. Gotlib, Ozlem Ayduk, Nicholas T. Franklin, Mary K. Askrend, John Jonides, et al. 2012. "Behavioral and neural correlates of delay of gratification 40 years later." *Annals of Neurosciences* 19 (1): 27–28. Accessed 10 11, 2018. https://experts.umich.edu/en/publications/behavioral-and-neural-correlates-of-delay-of-gratification-40-yea-2.

Chiba, Andrea. 2015. *Why we use rodents to research the brain.* April 2. https://www.sandiegouniontribune.com/news/science/sdut-brain-logic-behind-using-rodents-2015apr02-htmlstory.html.

Cognitive Neuroscience Society. 2013. *Why We So Often Blame the Person and Not the Situation.* November 20. https://www.cogneurosociety.org/fae_moran/.

Cook, Jennifer, Jennifer Cook, Hanneke E. M. den Ouden, Cecilia Heyes, and Roshan Cools. 2014. "The Social Dominance Paradox." *Current Biology* 24 (23): 2812–2816. Accessed 10 29, 2018. https://cell.com/current-biology/fulltext/s0960-9822(14)01290-1?code=cell-site.

Cooper, Robert. 2017. "#190 - Small Rules, Big Results." *UPWIRE.* Robert Cooper, February 23. https://player.fm/series/upwire-hacking-human-nature/upwire-190-small-rules-big-results.

Cooper, Robert. 2016. *UPWIRE #171 - Out Of The Blur.* June 3. http://robertcooper.libsyn.com/upwire-171-out-of-the-blur.

Cutting, James E., Jordan E. DeLong, and Christine E. Nothelfer. 2010. "Attention and the Evolution of Hollywood Film." *Psychological Science* 21 (3): 432–439. Accessed 10 17, 2018. http://people.psych.cornell.edu/~jec7/pubs/cuttingetalpsychsci10.pdf.

Darwin, Charles. 1872. The expression of emotions in man and animals.

Das, GD, and Altman Joseph. 1965. "Autoradiographic and Histological Evidence of Postnatal Hippocampal Neurogenesis in Rats." *Journal of Comparative Neurology* 124 (3): 319–35. Accessed 10 29, 2018.

Data Deluge. 2012. *The Unexpected Visitor* . October 4. http://www.datadeluge.com/2012/10/the-unexpected-visitor.html.

Dekker, Sanne, Nikki C. Lee, Paul A Howard-Jones, and Jelle Jolles. 2012. "Frontiers | Neuromyths in Education: Prevalence and ..." *Frontiers in Psychology* 3. Accessed 10 4, 2018. https://frontiersin.org/articles/10.3389/fpsyg.2012.00429/full.

DeSteno, David, Ye Li, Leah Dickens, and Jennifer S. Lerner. 2014. "Gratitude: A Tool for Reducing Economic Impatience." *Psychological Science* 25 (6): 1262-1267. Accessed 8 2, 2018. http://journals.sagepub.com/doi/abs/10.1177/0956797614529979.

DeWall, C. Nathan, Nathaniel M. Lambert, Richard S. Pond, Todd B. Kashdan, and Frank D. Fincham. 2012. "A Grateful Heart is a Nonviolent Heart Cross-Sectional, Experience Sampling, Longitudinal, and Experimental Evidence." *Social Psychological and Personality Science* 3 (2): 232-240. Accessed 8 1, 2018. http://journals.sagepub.com/doi/abs/10.1177/1948550611416675.

Diane F. Halpern, Milton D. Hakel. 2002. Applying the Science of Learning to the University and Beyond: Teaching for Long-Term Retention and Transfer. 1. Jossey-Bass.

Domenico, Stefano I. Di, and Richard M. Ryan. 2017. "The Emerging Neuroscience of Intrinsic Motivation: A New Frontier in Self-Determination Research." *Frontiers in Human Neuroscience* 11. Accessed 8 7, 2018. https://frontiersin.org/articles/10.3389/fnhum.2017.00145/full.

Domes, Gregor, Angela Steiner, Stephen W. Porges, and Markus Heinrichs. 2013. "Oxytocin differentially modulates eye gaze to naturalistic social signals of happiness and anger." *Psychoneuroendocrinology* 38 (7): 1198-1202. Accessed 7 10, 2018. https://ncbi.nlm.nih.gov/pubmed/23117026.

Ebbinghaus, Hermann. 2013. "Memory: A Contribution to Experimental Psychology." *Annals of Neuroscience* 20 (4): 155-156.

Edmondson, Amy C. 1999. "Psychological Safety and Learning Behavior in Work Teams." *Administrative Science Quarterly* 44 (2): 350-383. Accessed 11 9, 2018. http://journals.sagepub.com/doi/abs/10.2307/2666999.

Edwards, Jeffrey R., and Daniel M. Cable. 2009. "The Value of Value Congruence." *Journal of Applied Psychology* 94 (3): 654-677. Accessed 8 8, 2018. http://public.kenan-flagler.unc.edu/faculty/edwardsj/edwardscable2009.pdf.

Bra*in*sights

Eisenberger NI, Lieberman MD, Williams KD. 2003. "Does rejection hurt? An FMRI study of social exclusion." *Science* 302 (5643): 290–2. Accessed 10 21, 2018.

Eleanor A. Maguire, David G. Gadian, Ingrid S. Johnsrude, Catriona D. Good, John Ashburner, Richard S. J. Frackowiak, and Christopher D. Frith. 2000. "Navigation-related structural change in the hippocampi of taxi drivers." *PNAS* 16 (12): 4398–4403. doi:https://doi.org/10.1073/pnas.070039597.

Elle van Heusden, Martin Rolfs, Patrick Cavanagh and Hinze Hogendoorn. 2018. "Motion Extrapolation for Eye Movements Predicts Perceived Motion-Induced Position Shifts." *The Journal of Neuroscience* 8243–8250.

Elliot T Berkman, Jordan S Miller-Ziegler. 2013. "Imaging depletion: fMRI provides new insights into the processes underlying ego depletion." *Social Cognitive and Affective Neuroscience* 8 (4): 359–361. Accessed 7 3, 2018. https://ncbi.nlm.nih.gov/pmc/articles/pmc3624962.

Erskine, James A.K., George Georgiou, and Lia Kvavilashvili. 2010. "I Suppress, Therefore I Smoke Effects of Thought Suppression on Smoking Behavior." *Psychological Science* 21 (9): 1225-1230. Accessed 7 3, 2018. http://journals.sagepub.com/doi/full/10.1177/0956797610378687.

Esterman, Michael, Michael Esterman, Sarah Noonan, Monica D. Rosenberg, Joseph DeGutis, and Joseph DeGutis. 2011. "In the zone or zoning out? Tracking neural and behavioral fluctuations in visual attentional state." *F1000Research* 11 (11): 176-176. Accessed 8 29, 2018. http://jov.arvojournals.org/article.aspx?articleid=2139658.

Esterman, Michael, Sarah Noonan, Monica D. Rosenberg, and Joseph DeGutis. 2011. "In the zone or zoning out? Tracking neural and behavioral fluctuations in visual attentional state." *F1000Research* 2 (11): 176-176. Accessed 7 5, 2018. http://jov.arvojournals.org/article.aspx?articleid=2139658.

F. Sorrells, Shawn & Paredes, Mercedes & Cebrian-Silla, Arantxa & Sandoval, Kadellyn & Qi, Dashi & Kelley, Kevin & James, David & Mayer, Simone & Chang, Julia & I. Auguste, Kurtis & F. Chang, Edward & J. Gutierrez, Antonio & Kriegstein, Arnold & W. Mather. 2018. "Human hippocampal neurogenesis drops sharply in children to undetectable levels in adults." *Nature* 377-381.

Feinberg, Irwin. 2017. *Why Is Synaptic Pruning Important for the Developing Brain?* may 1. https://www.scientificamerican.com/article/why-is-synaptic-pruning-important-for-the-developing-brain/.

Feldman Barrett, Lisa. n.d. *How Emotions Are Made: The Secret Life of the Brain.* Houghton Mifflin Harcourt. Accessed 10 8, 2018. https://www.goodreads.com/book/show/23719305-how-emotions-are-made.

Fell, Juergen. 2012. "I think, therefore I am (unhappy)." *Frontiers in Human Neuroscience* 6: 132-132. Accessed 7 5, 2018. https://frontiersin.org/articles/10.3389/fnhum.2012.00132/full.

Flavell, John H. 1979. "Metacognition and cognitive monitoring: A new area of cognitive-developmental inquiry." *American Psychologist* 34 (10): 906-911. Accessed 7 5, 2018. http://psycnet.apa.org/psycinfo/1980-09388-001.

Forster, Daniel E., Eric J. Pedersen, Adam Smith, Michael E. McCullough, and Debra Lieberman. 2017. "Benefit valuation predicts gratitude." *Evolution and Human Behavior* 38 (1): 18-26. Accessed 7 31, 2018. https://sciencedirect.com/science/article/pii/s1090513816301131.

Fox, Glenn R., Jonas T. Kaplan, Hanna Damasio, and Antonio R. Damasio. 2015. "Neural correlates of gratitude." *Frontiers in Psychology* 6: 1491-1491. Accessed 7 31, 2018. https://ncbi.nlm.nih.gov/pmc/articles/pmc4588123.

Foxx, Dr. Glenn R., interview by Jesse Lawler. 2016. *What Gratitude Can Do For Your Brain* (August 19). https://smartdrugsmarts.com/episodes/episode-142-gratitude/.

Francesca Fortenbaugh, David Rothlein, Regina McGlinchey, Joseph DeGutis, Michael Estermanabce. 2018. "Tracking behavioral and neural fluctuations during sustained attention: A robust replication and extension." *NeuroImage* 171: 148-164. Accessed 7 5, 2018. https://sciencedirect.com/science/article/pii/s1053811918300028.

Freeman, Jonathan B., Ryan M. Stolier, Zachary A. Ingbretsen, and Eric Hehman. 2014. "Amygdala Responsivity to High-Level Social Information from Unseen Faces." *The Journal of Neuroscience* 34 (32): 10573-10581. Accessed 7 2, 2018. http://jneurosci.org/content/34/32/10573.

Friese, Malte, David D. Loschelder, Karolin Gieseler, Julius Frankenbach, and Michael Inzlicht. 2018. "Is Ego Depletion Real? An Analysis of Arguments:." *Personality and Social Psychology Review* 108886831876218. Accessed 10 26, 2018. http://journals.sagepub.com/doi/abs/10.1177/1088868318762183.

G. Domes, M. Heinrichs, A. Michel, C. Berger, SC Herpertz. 2007. "Oxytocin improves "mind-reading" in humans." *Biological Psychiatry* 61 (6): 731-3. Accessed 7 30, 2018.

Giacomo Rizzolatti, Luciano Fadiga, Leonardo Fogassi, G.Pavesi. 1995. "Motor Facilitation During Action Observation: A Magnetic Stimulation Study." *Journal of Neurophysiology* 73 (6): 2608-2611. Accessed 8 27, 2018. http://wexler.free.fr/library/files/fadiga (1995) motor facilitation during action observation. a magnetic stimulation study.pdf.

Gibbens, Sarah. 2018. *Memories Can Be Altered in Mice. Are Humans Next?* July 13. https://www.nationalgeographic.com/science/2018/07/news-memory-manipulation-research-neuroscience/.

Glaser, Judith E. 2013. Conversational Intelligence: How great leaders build trust and get extraordinary results. New York: Routledge.

Glenn R. Fox, Jonas Kaplan, Hanna Damasio, Antonio Damasio. 2015. "Neural correlates of gratitude." *Frontiers in Psychology*, September 30. https://www.frontiersin.org/articles/10.3389/fpsyg.2015.01491/full.

n.d. *Global IQ: 1950–2050*. https://www.fourmilab.ch/documents/IQ/1950-2050/.

Goldstein, Elisha. 2018. *Elisha Goldstein, Ph.D.* April 24. https://elishagoldstein.com/the-neuroscience-of-bad-habits-and-why-its-not-about-will-power/.

Gosen, Jerry, and John Washbush. 2004. "A Review of Scholarship on Assessing Experiential Learning Effectiveness." *Simulation & Gaming* 35 (2): 270-293. Accessed 10 15, 2018. http://journals.sagepub.com/doi/abs/10.1177/1046878104263544.

Gow, Iain. 2012. "Thinking Fast and Slow." *The Innovation Journal* 17 (3): 1. Accessed 6 29, 2018. https://questia.com/library/journal/1p3-2990074911/thinking-fast-and-slow.

Greg J Stephens, Lauren J. Silbert, Uri Hasson. 2010. "Speaker-listener neural coupling underlies successful communication." *Proceedings of the National Academy of Sciences of the United States of America* 107 (32): 14425-14430. Accessed 8 27, 2018. http://pnas.org/content/107/32/14425.

Gregersen, Hal. 2018. "Better Brainstorming." *Harvard Business Review*, March-April. https://hbr.org/2018/03/better-brainstorming.

Groot, A.N.J.A. de, T. B. Vree, Y.A. Hekster, G.J. Pesman, F.C.G.J. Sweep, P.W.J. van Dongen, and J. van Roosmalen. 1995. "Bioavailability and Pharmacokinetics of Sublingual Oxytocin in Male Volunteers." *Journal of Pharmacy and Pharmacology* 47 (7): 571-575. Accessed 7 10, 2018. http://onlinelibrary.wiley.com/doi/10.1111/j.2042-7158.1995.tb06716.x/abstract.

Guglielmi, Giorgia. 2018. "Neuron creation in brain's memory centre stops after childhood." *Nature.* March 7. https://www.nature.com/articles/d41586-018-02812-6.

Habib, Reza, and Mark R. Dixon. 2010. "Neurobehavioral Evidence for the "Near-Miss" Effect in Pathological Gamblers." *Journal of the Experimental Analysis of Behavior* 93 (3): 313-328. Accessed 10 23, 2018. http://onlinelibrary.wiley.com/doi/10.1901/jeab.2010.93-313/full.

Hagura, Nobuhiro, Patrick Haggard, and Jörn Diedrichsen. 2017. "Correction: Perceptual decisions are biased by the cost to act." *eLife* 6. Accessed 6 26, 2018. https://elifesciences.org/articles/26902.

Harlow, John M. 1850. "RECOVERY AFTER SEVERE INJURY TO THE HEAD." *Massachusetts Medical Society.* Boston : DAVID CLAPP & SON 334 WASHINGTON STREET. 13-22. https://archive.org/stream/66210360R.nlm.nih.gov/66210360R_djvu.txt.

Hartley, Catherine A., and Leah H. Somerville. 2015. "The neuroscience of adolescent decision-making." *Current opinion in behavioral sciences* 5: 108-115. Accessed 10 20, 2018. https://ncbi.nlm.nih.gov/pmc/articles/pmc4671080.

Harvard Health Publishing. 2011. *Understanding the stress response: Chronic activation of this survival mechanism impairs health.* March. https://www.health.harvard.edu/staying-healthy/understanding-the-stress-response.

Hasenkamp, Wendy, and Lawrence W. Barsalou. 2012. "Effects of Meditation Experience on Functional Connectivity of Distributed Brain Networks." *Frontiers in Human Neuroscience* 6 (38): 38-38. Accessed 10 5, 2018. http://journal.frontiersin.org/article/10.3389/fnhum.2012.00038/full.

Herculano-Houzel, Suzana. 2009. "The human brain in numbers: a linearly scaled-up primate brain." *Frontiers in Human Neuroscience* 3: 31-31. Accessed 8 13, 2018. http://cogs.indiana.edu/spackled/2010readings/herculano-houzel_human brain in numbers_2009.pdf.

Herrero, Jose Luis, Jose Luis Herrero, Simon Khuvis, Erin Yeagle, Moran Cerf, and Ashesh D. Mehta. 2018. "Breathing above the brain stem: volitional control and attentional modulation in humans." *Journal of Neurophysiology* 119 (1): 145-159. Accessed 10 9, 2018. https://physiology.org/doi/10.1152/jn.00551.2017.

Hobson, Katherine. 2018. *Clicking: How Our Brains Are in Sync .* April 11. https://paw.princeton.edu/article/clicking-how-our-brains-are-sync.

Bra*in*sights

Howard P. Roffwarg, Joseph N. Muzio, William C. Dement. 1966. "Ontogenetic Development of the Human Sleep-Dream Cycle." *Science* 152 (3722): 604-619. Accessed 7 5, 2018. http://science.sciencemag.org/content/152/3722/604.

Hsu, David T., Benjamin J Sanford, Kortni K. Meyers, Tiffany Love, Kathleen Hazlett, Heng Wang, Lisong Ni, et al. 2013. "Response of the μ-opioid system to social rejection and acceptance." *Molecular Psychiatry* 18 (11): 1211-1217. Accessed 10 21, 2018. https://ncbi.nlm.nih.gov/pubmed/23958960.

Immordino-Yang, Mary Helen, Joanna A. Christodoulou, and Vanessa Singh. 2012. "Rest Is Not Idleness Implications of the Brain's Default Mode for Human Development and Education." *Perspectives on Psychological Science* 7 (4): 352-364. Accessed 7 4, 2018. http://journals.sagepub.com/doi/abs/10.1177/1745691612447308.

Inzlicht, Michael. 2018. "The Toronto Laboratory for Social Neuroscience explores the science of self-control." *Michael Inzlicht.* http://michaelinzlicht.com/research.

J Tiago Gonçalves, Cooper W Bloyd, Matthew Shtrahman, Stephen T Johnston, Simon T Schafer, Sarah L Parylak, Thanh Tran, Tina Chang & Fred H Gage. 2016. "In vivo imaging of dendritic pruning in dentate granule cells." *Nature Neuroscience 19* 788-791.

Jackowska, Marta, Jennie Brown, Amy Ronaldson, and Andrew Steptoe. 2016. "The impact of a brief gratitude intervention on subjective well-being, biology and sleep." *Journal of Health Psychology* 21 (10): 2207-2217. Accessed 8 1, 2018. http://journals.sagepub.com/doi/abs/10.1177/1359105315572455.

Janine Willis, Alexander Todorov. 2006. "Making Up Your Mind After a 100-Ms Exposure to a Face." *Psychological Science* 592-598.

Jeffrey A. Brooks, Holly Shablack, Maria Gendron, Ajay B. Satpute, Michael H. Parrish, and Kristen A. Lindquist. 2017. "The role of language in the experience and perception of emotion: a neuroimaging meta-analysis ." *Social Cognitive and Affective Neuroscience* 169-183.

Joel|Joel, Daphna|Daphna, and Cordelia Fine|et al. n.d. *Sex beyond the genitalia: The human brain mosaic.* Accessed 6 26, 2018. https://doi.org/10.1073/pnas.1509654112.

Josef Sadowski, Matthew W. Jones, Jack R. Mellor. 2016. "Sharp-Wave Ripples Orchestrate the Induction of Synaptic Plasticity during Reactivation of Place Cell Firing Patterns in the Hippocampus." *Cell Reports* 14 (8): 1916-1929.

Accessed 7 5, 2018. http://cell.com/cell-reports/fulltext/s2211-1247(16)30039-0.

Kahn, WA. 1990. "Psychological Conditions of Personal Engagement and Disengagement at Work." *Academy of Management Journal* (33): 692--724. doi:10.2307/256287.

Kahneman, Daniel. 2011. *Thinking Fast and Slow.* New Yourk: Farrar, Straus and Giroux. Accessed 8 29, 2018.

Karns, Christina M., William E. Moore, and Ulrich Mayr. 2017. "The Cultivation of Pure Altruism via Gratitude: A Functional MRI Study of Change with Gratitude Practice." *Frontiers in Human Neuroscience* 11. Accessed 11 15, 2018. https://frontiersin.org/articles/10.3389/fnhum.2017.00599/full.

Kathryn W. Brady, Judith C. Goodman. 2014. "The Type, but Not the Amount, of Information Available Influences Toddlers' Fast Mapping and Retention of New Words." *American Journal of Speech-Language Pathology* 120-133.

Kelley, Paul, and Terry Whatson. 2013. "Making long-term memories in minutes: a spaced learning pattern from memory research in education." *Frontiers in Human Neuroscience* 7: 589-589. Accessed 10 3, 2018. https://frontiersin.org/articles/10.3389/fnhum.2013.00589/full.

Kevin Yackle, Lindsay A. Schwarz, Kaiwen Kam, Jordan M. Sorokin, John R. Huguenard, Jack L. Feldman, Liqun Luo, Mark A. Krasnow. 2017. "Breathing control center neurons that promote arousal in mice." *Science* 355: 1411-1415.

Killingsworth MA, Gilbert DT. n.d. "A wandering mind is an unhappy mind." *Science* 330 (6006): 932. Accessed 7 5, 2018.

Kini, P., Wong, J., McInnis, S., Gabana, N., and Brown, J. W. 2016. "The effects of gratitude expression on neural activity." *Neuroimage* 1-10. doi:10.1016/j.neuroimage.2015.12.040.

Kirsty L. Spalding, Olaf Bergmann, Kanar Alkass, Samuel Bernard, Mehran Salehpour, Hagen B. Huttner, Emil Boström, Isabelle Westerlund, Céline Vial, Bruce A. Buchholz, Göran Possnert, Deborah C. Mash, Henrik Druid, Jonas Frisén. 2013. "Dynamics of Hippocampal Neurogenesis in Adult Humans." *Cell* 219-1227.

Knutson, Brian, G. Elliott Wimmer, Camelia M. Kuhnen, and Piotr Winkielman. 2008. *Nucleus accumbens activation mediates the influence of reward cues on financial risk-taking.* Accessed 10 22, 2018. https://ideas.repec.org/p/pra/mprapa/8013.html.

Kolb, David A. 1984. Experiential Learning: Experience as the Source of Learning and Development. Englewood Cliffs, NJ: Prentice-Hall.

Koti, Shruti. 2014. "Fear: a Blessing and Curse." *Berkeley Scientific Journal* 19 (1). Accessed 8 15, 2018. https://escholarship.org/uc/item/9cp6x7nd.

Kragel, Philip A., Nancy Zucker, Virginia E. Covington, and Kevin S. LaBar. 2015. "Developmental trajectories of cortical-subcortical interactions underlying the evaluation of trust in adolescence." *Social Cognitive and Affective Neuroscience* 10 (2): 240-247. Accessed 10 20, 2018. https://ncbi.nlm.nih.gov/pmc/articles/pmc4321625.

Kyle S. Smithc, Ann M. Graybiel. 2016. "Habit formation coincides with shifts in reinforcement representations in the sensorimotor striatum." *Journal of Neurophysiology* 1487-1498.

Lally, Phillippa, Cornelia H.M. van Jaarsveld, Henry W. W. Potts, and Jane Wardle. 2010. "How are habits formed: Modelling habit formation in the real world." *European Journal of Social Psychology* 40 (6): 998-1009. Accessed 8 31, 2018. https://onlinelibrary.wiley.com/doi/abs/10.1002/ejsp.674.

Lawler, Jesse. 2018. *#220: COGNITIVE FALLACIES WITH DR. RICHARD E. NISBETT.* March 02. https://smartdrugsmarts.com/episodes/220-errors-richard-nisbett/.

Lebreton, Mael, Mael Lebreton, Maxime Bertoux, Claire Boutet, Claire Boutet, Stéphane Lehéricy, Stéphane Lehéricy, et al. 2013. "A critical role for the hippocampus in the valuation of imagined outcomes." *PLOS Biology* 11 (10). Accessed 10 23, 2018. http://journals.plos.org/plosbiology/article?id=10.1371/journal.pbio.1001684.

Ledford, Heidi. 2008. "'Monogamous' vole in love-rat shock." *Nature* 617.

LeDoux, Joseph E. 2000. *The amygdala and emotion: a view through fear.* Oxford: Oxford University Press.

—. 2015. *The Amygdala Is NOT the Brain's Fear Center.* August 10. https://www.psychologytoday.com/intl/blog/i-got-mind-tell-you/201508/the-amygdala-is-not-the-brains-fear-center.

Lewis, Tanya. 2014. *A Beautiful Mind: Brain Injury Turns Man Into Math Genius.* May 5. https://www.livescience.com/45349-brain-injury-turns-man-into-math-genius.html.

Libet, Benjamin, Curtis A. Gleason, Elwood W. Wright, and Dennis K. Pearl. 1983. "TIME OF CONSCIOUS INTENTION TO ACT IN RELATION TO

ONSET OF CEREBRAL ACTIVITY (READINESS-POTENTIAL)THE UNCONSCIOUS INITIATION OF A FREELY VOLUNTARY ACT." *Brain* 106 (3): 623-642. Accessed 10 31, 2018. https://philpapers.org/rec/libtoc-3.

Lilli Kimppa, Teija Kujala & Yury Shtyrov. 2016. "Individual language experience modulates rapid formation of cortical memory circuits for novel words." *Scientific Reports.* https://www.nature.com/articles/srep30227.

Lindgaard, Gitte, Gary Fernandes, Cathy Dudek, and Judith M. Brown. 2006. "Attention web designers: You have 50 milliseconds to make a good first impression!" *Behaviour & Information Technology* 25 (2): 115-126. Accessed 7 2, 2018. http://tandfonline.com/doi/abs/10.1080/01449290500330448.

Lindvall, Olle, and Zaal Kokaia. 2015. "Neurogenesis following Stroke Affecting the Adult Brain." *Cold Spring Harbor Perspectives in Biology* 7 (11): 019034-019034. Accessed 10 22, 2018. http://cshperspectives.cshlp.org/content/7/11/a019034.short.

Linnet, Jakob, Jakob Linnet, Kim Mouridsen, Ericka Peterson, Ericka Peterson, Arne Møller, Arne Møller, et al. 2012. "Striatal dopamine release codes uncertainty in pathological gambling." *Psychiatry Research-neuroimaging* 204 (1): 55-60. Accessed 8 30, 2018. https://ncbi.nlm.nih.gov/pubmed/22889563.

Loftus, E. 1997. "Creating False Memories - University of Washington." *Scientific American* 227 (3): 71-75. Accessed 9 5, 2018. https://faculty.washington.edu/eloftus/Articles/sciam.htm.

Loftus, E. 1993. "The Reality of Repressed Memories." *The American Psychologist* 48 (5): 518-537. Accessed 10 4, 2018. http://faculty.washington.edu/eloftus/Articles/lof93.htm.

Lorie G. Richards, Kim C. Stewart, Michelle L. Woodbury, Claudia Senesac, and James H. Cauraugh. 2008. "Movement-Dependent Stroke Recovery: A Systematic Review and Meta-Analysis of TMS and fMRI Evidence." *Neuropsychologia* 3-11. doi:10.1016/j.neuropsychologia.2007.08.013.

Lotto, Beau, interview by Georgia Frances King. 2017. *A neuroscientist explains why we can't see the world objectively—and humanity is better for it* Quartz, (May 3). https://qz.com/973116/a-neuroscientist-explains-why-we-evolved-to-be-curious/.

Lufityanto, Galang, Chris Donkin, and Joel Pearson. 2016. "Measuring Intuition: Nonconscious Emotional Information Boosts Decision Accuracy and

Confidence." *Psychological Science* 27 (5): 622-634. Accessed 8 15, 2018. http://journals.sagepub.com/doi/abs/10.1177/0956797616629403.

Luisa de Vivo, Michele Bellesi, William Marshall, Eric A. Bushong, Mark H. Ellisman, Giulio Tononi, Chiara Cirelli. 2017. "Ultrastructural evidence for synaptic scaling across the wake/sleep cycle." *Science* 355 (6324): 507-510.

Lyle, Henry F., and Eric Alden Smith. 2014. "The reputational and social network benefits of prosociality in an Andean community." *Proceedings of the National Academy of Sciences of the United States of America* 111 (13): 4820-4825. Accessed 11 8, 2018. http://pnas.org/content/111/13/4820.short.

M Mauraven, RF Baumeister. 2000. "Self-regulation and depletion of limited resources: does self-control resemble a muscle?" *Psychological bulletin 126 2* 247-59.

M. Altmann, Erik & Gregory Trafton, J & Hambrick, Zach. 2017. "Effects of Interruption Length on Procedural Errors." *Journal of Experimental Psychology: Applied.*

M. Iacoboni, RP Woods, M. Brass, H. Bekkering, JC Mazziotta, G Rizzolatti. 1999. "Cortical Mechanisms of Human Imitation." *Science* 286 (5449): 2526-8. Accessed 8 27, 2018.

Macknik, S.L., et al., King M, Randi J, Apollo Robbins, Teller, John Thompson, and Susana Martinez-Conde. n.d. "Attention and Awareness in Stage Magic: Turning Tricks into Research." *Nat. Rev. Neurosci.* 9 (11): 871-9. Accessed 10 15, 2018.

Malini Suchak, Timothy M. Eppley, Matthew W. Campbell, Rebecca A. Feldman, Luke F. Quarles, Frans B. M. de Waal. 2016. "How chimpanzees cooperate in a competitive world." *Proceedings of the National Academy of Sciences*, August 17. http://www.pnas.org/content/early/2016/08/16/1611826113.full.pdf.

Mark Bolino, David Long, and William Turnley. 2016. "Impression Management in Organizations: Critical Questions, Answers, and Areas for Future Research." *The Annual Review of Organizational Psychology and Organizational Behavior* . January 6. https://www.annualreviews.org/doi/abs/10.1146/annurev-orgpsych-041015-062337.

Mark, Gloria, Victor M. Gonzalez, and Justin Harris. 2005. *No task left behind?: examining the nature of fragmented work.* Accessed 8 9, 2018. https://ics.uci.edu/~gmark/chi2005.pdf.

Martin A Nowak, Sébastien Roch. 2007. "Upstream reciprocity and the evolution of gratitude." *Proceedings of the Royal Society B: Biological Sciences*, March 4: 605-610. doi:10.1098/rspb.2006.0125.

Mary Helen Immordino-Yang, Joanna A Christodoulou, Vanessa Singh,. 2012. "Rest Is Not Idleness Implications of the Brain's Default Mode for Human Development and Education." *Perspectives on Psychological Science* 7 (4): 352-364. Accessed 7 4, 2018. http://journals.sagepub.com/doi/abs/10.1177/1745691612447308.

Matthias Ekman, Peter Kok, Floris P. de Lange. 2017. "Time-compressed preplay of anticipated events in human primary visual cortex." *Nature Communications* 8.

McCollister, John. 2005. Tales from the 1979 Pittsburgh Pirates: Remembering "The Fam-A-Lee". Sports Publishing LLC.

Mead, N. L., Baumeister, R. F., Stuppy, A., & Vohs, K. D. 2018. "Power increases the socially toxic component of narcissism among individuals with high baseline testosterone." *Journal of Experimental Psychology: General* 147 (4): 591-596.

Mehlman, Maxwell J. 2004. "Cognition-Enhancing Drugs." *Milbank Quarterly* 82 (3): 483-506. Accessed 11 29, 2018. https://ncbi.nlm.nih.gov/pmc/articles/pmc2690227.

Michael Inzlicht, Elliot Berkman & Nathaniel Elkins-Brown. 2016. "The neuroscience of "ego depletion" or: How the brain can help us understand why selfcontrol seems limited." *Michael Inzlicht.* http://michaelinzlicht.com/publications/articles-chapters/the-neuroscience-of-ego-depletion-or-how-the-brain-can-help-us-understand-why-self-control-seems-limited-pdf.

—. 2016. "The neuroscience of "ego depletion" or: How the brain can help us understand why selfcontrol seems limited." *Michael Inzlicht.* http://michaelinzlicht.com/publications/articles-chapters/the-neuroscience-of-ego-depletion-or-how-the-brain-can-help-us-understand-why-self-control-seems-limited-pdf.

Michael Kosfeld, Markus Heinrichs, Paul J Zak, Urs Fischbacher, Ernst Fehr. 2005. "Oxytocin Increases Trust in Humans." *Nature* 435 (7042): 673-676. Accessed 7 30, 2018. http://dept.wofford.edu/neuroscience/neuroseminar/pdffall2008/oxy-human.pdf.

Michelle E. Stepan, Kimberly M. Fenn, Erik M. Altmann. 2018. "Effects of sleep deprivation on procedural errors." *Journal of Experimental Psychology: General* No Pagination Specified.

Miller, George A. 1955. "The Magical Number Seven, Plus or Minus Two Some Limits on Our Capacity for Processing Information." *Psychological Review* 101 (No. 2): 343-352.

Mischel, Walter. 2014. The Marshmallow Test: Mastering Self-Control. Little, Brown Spark.

Mischel, Walter, Ebbe B. Ebbesen, and Antonette Raskoff Zeiss. 1972. "Cognitive and Attentional Mechanisms in Delay of Gratification." *Journal of Personality and Social Psychology* 21 (2): 204-218. Accessed 10 11, 2018. http://viriya.net/jabref/cognitive_and_attentional_mechanisms_in_delay_of_g ratification.pdf.

Moran, Joseph M., Eshin Jolly, and Jason P. Mitchell. 2014. "Spontaneous mentalizing predicts the fundamental attribution error." *Journal of Cognitive Neuroscience* 26 (3): 569-576. Accessed 8 31, 2018. https://dash.harvard.edu/bitstream/handle/1/13457155/jocn_a_00513.pdf?s equence=1.

Morris, Adam P., Charles C. Liu, Simon J. Cropper, Jason D. Forte, Bart Krekelberg, and Jason B. Mattingley. 2010. "Summation of Visual Motion across Eye Movements Reflects a Nonspatial Decision Mechanism." *The Journal of Neuroscience* 30 (29): 9821-9830. Accessed 10 31, 2018. https://ncbi.nlm.nih.gov/pmc/articles/pmc2917252.

Morris, Michael. 2012. *Boo! Unto Others.* January 19. https://biblefunmentionables.wordpress.com/2012/01/19/boo-unto-others/.

Mulholland, Patrick J., Tara Teppen, Kelsey M. Miller, Hannah G. Sexton, Subhash C. Pandey, and H. Scott Swartzwelder. 2018. "Donepezil Reverses Dendritic Spine Morphology Adaptations and Fmr1 Epigenetic Modifications in Hippocampus of Adult Rats After Adolescent Alcohol Exposure." *Alcoholism: Clinical and Experimental Research* 42 (4): 706-717. Accessed 11 15, 2018. https://uic.pure.elsevier.com/en/publications/donepezil-reverses-dendritic-spine-morphology-adaptations-and-fmr.

Mulukom, Valerie van. 2018. *Is It Rational to Trust Your Gut Feelings?* May 18. http://neurosciencenews.com/gut-feelings-9082.

Nadler, Relly. 2011. *Where Did My IQ points Go?* . April 29. https://www.psychologytoday.com/us/blog/leading-emotional-intelligence/201104/where-did-my-iq-points-go.

Nelson, Justin, Richard A. McKinley, Chandler A. Phillips, Lindsey McIntire, Chuck Goodyear, Aerial Kreiner, and Lanie Monforton. 2016. "The Effects of Transcranial Direct Current Stimulation (tDCS) on Multitasking Throughput Capacity." *Frontiers in Human Neuroscience* 10. Accessed 11 27, 2018. https://frontiersin.org/articles/10.3389/fnhum.2016.00589/full.

Nilsson M, Perfilieva E, Johansson U, Orwar O, Eriksson PS. 1999. "Enriched environment increases neurogenesis in the adult rat dentate gyrus and improves spatial memory." *Journal of Neurobiology* 569-78.

Nottebohm, Fernando. 1989. "From bird song to neurogenesis." *Scientific American* 260 (2): 74-79. Accessed 10 29, 2018. http://nature.com/doifinder/10.1038/scientificamerican0289-74.

Novembre, Giovanni, Marco Zanon, and Giorgia Silani. 2015. "Empathy for social exclusion involves the sensory-discriminative component of pain: a within-subject fMRI study." *Social Cognitive and Affective Neuroscience* 10 (2): 153-164. Accessed 8 28, 2018. https://academic.oup.com/scan/article/10/2/153/1652379.

Nowak, M. A., and S Roch. 2007. "Upstream reciprocity and the evolution of gratitude." *Proceedings of the Royal Society B: Biological Sciences* 274 (1610): 605-610. Accessed 7 31, 2018.

Nowak, Martin A., and Sebastien Roch. 2007. *Upstream reciprocity and the evolution of gratitude.* Accessed 7 31, 2018. https://ncbi.nlm.nih.gov/pmc/articles/pmc2197219.

Oberman, Lindsay M., and Jaime A. Pineda. 2007. "The human mirror neuron system: A link between action observation and social skills." *Social Cognitive and Affective Neuroscience* 2 (1): 62-66. Accessed 6 26, 2018. https://ncbi.nlm.nih.gov/pmc/articles/pmc2555434.

Olds, James, and Peter Milner. 1954. "Positive reinforcement produced by electrical stimulation of septal area and other regions of rat brain." *Journal of Comparative and Physiological Psychology* 47 (6): 419-427. Accessed 8 3, 2018. https://ncbi.nlm.nih.gov/pubmed/13233369.

Ophir, Eyal, Clifford Nass, and Anthony D. Wagner. 2009. "Cognitive control in media multitaskers." *Proceedings of the National Academy of Sciences of the United States of America* 106 (37): 15583-15587. Accessed 7 9, 2018. http://pnas.org/content/106/37/15583.

2018. *Oxytocin Pair Bonding - Oxytocin Basics.* https://www.psychologytoday.com/intl/basics/oxytocin.

Papies, Esther K., and Henk Aarts. 2016. Automatic self-regulation: From habit to goal pursuit : Handbook of self regulation: Research, theory, and applications. Accessed 10 5, 2018. https://dspace.library.uu.nl/handle/1874/346281.

Pashler, Harold, Mark A. McDaniel, Doug Rohrer, and Robert A. Bjork. 2008. "Learning Styles Concepts and Evidence." *Psychological Science in the Public Interest* 9 (3): 105-119. Accessed 10 4, 2018. http://journals.sagepub.com/doi/abs/10.1111/j.1539-6053.2009.01038.x.

Paul Ekman, Wallace V. Friesen. 1971. "Constants Across Cultures in the Face and Emotion." *Journal of Personality and Social Psychology* 17 (2): 124-129.

Paul J Zak, Jorge A Barraza. 2013. "The neurobiology of collective action." *Frontiers in Neuroscience* 7: 211-211. Accessed 7 30, 2018. https://ncbi.nlm.nih.gov/pmc/articles/pmc3832785.

Paul J. Zak, Robert Kurzban, Sheila Ahmadi, Ronald S. Swerdloff, Jang Park, Levan Efremidze, Karen Redwine, Karla Morgan, William Matzner. 2009. "Testosterone Administration Decreases Generosity in the Ultimatum Game." *PLoS ONE* 4 (12). https://doi.org/10.1371/journal.pone.0008330.

Payne, Jessica D. 2011. "Learning, Memory, and Sleep in Humans." *Sleep Medicine Clinics* 6 (1): 15-30. Accessed 7 4, 2018. http://sciencedirect.com/science/article/pii/s1556407x10001220.

Payne, Jessica D., Eric D. Jackson, Lee Ryan, Siobhan Hoscheidt, W. Jake Jacobs, and Lynn Nadel. 2006. "The impact of stress on neutral and emotional aspects of episodic memory." *Memory* 14 (1): 1-16. Accessed 10 2, 2018. http://tandfonline.com/doi/abs/10.1080/09658210500139176.

Petersson, Maria, Kerstin Uvnäs-Moberg, Anne Nilsson, Lise-Lotte Gustafson, Eva Hydbring-Sandberg, and Linda Handlin. 2017. "Oxytocin and Cortisol Levels in Dog Owners and Their Dogs Are Associated with Behavioral Patterns : An Exploratory Study." *Frontiers in Psychology* 8. Accessed 7 10, 2018. https://frontiersin.org/articles/10.3389/fpsyg.2017.01796/full.

Pierson, David. 2017. "Reengineering Army Education for Adult Learners." *Journal of Military Learning* 6/11.

Poudel, Govinda R., Govinda R. Poudel, Carrie R. H. Innes, Philip J. Bones, Richard Watts, and Richard D. Jones. 2014. "Losing the struggle to stay awake: Divergent thalamic and cortical activity during microsleeps." *Human Brain Mapping* 35 (1): 257-269. Accessed 10 19, 2018.

http://nzbri.org/resources/publications/134/poudel_human_brain_mapping_2014.pdf.

Prouska, Rea, and Alexandros G. Psychogios. 2018. "Do not say a word! Conceptualizing employee silence in a long-term crisis context." *International Journal of Human Resource Management* 29 (5): 885-914. Accessed 11 8, 2018. http://tandfonline.com/doi/full/10.1080/09585192.2016.1212913.

Pychyl, Timothy A. 2013. *Solving the Procrastination Puzzle: A Concise Guide to Strategies for Change.* Accessed 7 5, 2018. https://amazon.com/solving-procrastination-puzzle-concise-strategies/dp/0399168125.

Raam, Tara, Kathleen M. McAvoy, Antoine Besnard, Alexa H. Veenema, and Amar Sahay. 2017. "Hippocampal oxytocin receptors are necessary for discrimination of social stimuli." *Nature Communications* 8 (1): 2001. Accessed 7 11, 2018. http://nature.com/articles/s41467-017-02173-0.

Radulovic, Jelena, and Natalie C. Tronson. 2011. "Receptors in (e)motion." *Nature Neuroscience* 14 (10): 1222-1224. Accessed 7 11, 2018. http://nature.com/neuro/journal/v14/n10/fig_tab/nn.2938_f1.html.

Raichle, Marcus E., and Debra A. Gusnard. 2002. "Appraising the brain's energy budget." *Proceedings of the National Academy of Sciences of the United States of America* 99 (16): 10237-10239. Accessed 10 31, 2018. http://pnas.org/content/99/16/10237.

Razorfish. 2015. *Digital Dopamine.* Razorfish, 27.

Ring, Karen. 2016. *An inside look reveals the adult brain prunes its own branches.* May 2. https://blog.cirm.ca.gov/2016/05/02/an-inside-look-reveals-the-adult-brain-prunes-its-own-branches/.

Rolfs, Martin, Donatas Jonikaitis, Heiner Deubel, and Patrick Cavanagh. 2011. "Predictive remapping of attention across eye movements." *Nature Neuroscience* 14 (2): 252-256. Accessed 10 24, 2018. http://cavlab.net/wp-content/uploads/2009/07/rolfseal_predictive-remapping_natureneuro2011.pdf.

Rolls, Edmund T. 2016. *Brain Processing of Reward for Touch, Temperature, and Oral Texture.* Accessed 11 9, 2018. https://link.springer.com/content/pdf/10.1007/978-1-4939-6418-5_13.pdf.

Rubinstein, Joshua S., David E. Meyer, and Jeffrey E. Evans. 2001. "Executive Control of Cognitive Processes in Task Switching." *Journal of Experimental Psychology: Human Perception and Performance* 27 (4): 763-797. Accessed 7 9, 2018. http://apa.org/pubs/journals/releases/xhp274763.pdf.

S. Chennu, V. Noreika, D. Gueorguiev, A. Blenkmann, S. Kochen, A. Ibáñez, A. M. Owen, and T. A. Bekinschtein. 2013. "Expectation and attention in hierarchical auditory prediction." *The Journal of Neuroscience* 33 (27): 11194-11205.

Sacks, Oliver. 2003. *A Bolt from the Blue - Where do sudden intense passions come from?* July 23. https://www.newyorker.com/magazine/2007/07/23/a-bolt-from-the-blue.

Sadowski, Josef, Matthew W. Jones, and Jack R. Mellor. 2016. "Sharp-Wave Ripples Orchestrate the Induction of Synaptic Plasticity during Reactivation of Place Cell Firing Patterns in the Hippocampus." *Cell Reports* 14 (8): 1916-1929. Accessed 10 19, 2018. https://sciencedirect.com/science/article/pii/s2211124716300390.

Salamone JD, Correa M. 2012. "The Mysterious Motivational Functions of Mesolimbic Dopamine." *Neuron* 76 (3): 470–485. Accessed 10 23, 2018.

Salk Institute. 2007. *Associative Memory -- Learning At All Levels.* March 15. www.sciencedaily.com/releases/2007/03/070314134812.htm.

Sapolsky, Robert. 2017. Behave: The Biology of Humans at Our Best and Worst. Penguin Press.

Sapolsky, Robert M. 2017. Behave: The Biology of Humans at Our Best and Worst. Penguin Books.

Scheele D, Striepens N, Güntürkün O, Deutschländer S, Maier W, Kendrick KM, Hurlemann R. 2012. "Oxytocin modulates social distance between males and females." *The Journal of Neuroscience* 32 (46): 16074-9. Accessed 7 10, 2018.

Scheele, Dirk, Andrea Wille, Keith M. Kendrick, Birgit Stoffel-Wagner, Benjamin Becker, Onur Güntürkün, Wolfgang Maier, and René Hurlemann. 2013. "Oxytocin enhances brain reward system responses in men viewing the face of their female partner." *Proceedings of the National Academy of Sciences of the United States of America* 110 (50): 20308-20313. Accessed 7 10, 2018. http://pnas.org/content/110/50/20308.abstract.

Schmelzer, Gretchen. 2015. *Gretchen Schmelzer.* January 11. http://gretchenschmelzer.com/blog-1/2015/1/11/understanding-learning-and-memory-the-neuroscience-of-repetition.

—. 2015. *Understanding Learning and Memory: The Neuroscience of Repetition.* January 11. http://gretchenschmelzer.com/blog-1/2015/1/11/understanding-learning-and-memory-the-neuroscience-of-repetition.

Schneiderman, Inna, Orna Zagoory-Sharon, James F. Leckman, and Ruth Feldman. 2012. "Oxytocin during the initial stages of romantic attachment: Relations to couples' interactive reciprocity." *Psychoneuroendocrinology* 37 (8): 1277-1285. Accessed 7 31, 2018. https://sciencedirect.com/science/article/pii/s0306453012000029.

Schultz, Wolfram. 2017. "Reward prediction error." *Current Biology* 27 (10). Accessed 6 25, 2018. http://cell.com/current-biology/fulltext/s0960-9822(17)30266-x.

Schwartz, Casey. 2015. "A Neuroscientist Argues That Everybody Is Misunderstanding Fear and Anxiety." *The Cut.* July 23. https://www.thecut.com/2015/07/everybody-misunderstanding-fear-and-anxiety.html.

n.d. *Science of Gratitude.* Accessed 8 1, 2018. http://gratitudepower.net/science.htm.

Scott D. Anthony, S. Patrick Viguerie, Evan I. Schwartz and John Van Landeghem. 2015. https://www.innosight.com/insight/creative-destruction/.

Seth, Dr. Anil, interview by Jesse Lawler. 2018. *#228: Perception as a Controlled Hallucination* (May 28).

Shalvia, S., and C. K. W. De Dreu. 2014. "Oxytocin promotes group-serving dishonesty." *Proceedings of the National Academy of Sciences of the United States of America* 111: 5503-5507. Accessed 7 30, 2018.

Shinoda, Tomohito. 2013. "DPJ's Political Leadership in Response to the Fukushima Nuclear Accident." *Japanese Journal of Political Science* 14 (02): 243-259. Accessed 8 20, 2018. http://journals.cambridge.org/action/displayfulltext?type=1&fid=8912075&volumeid=14&issueid=02&aid=8912073&bodyid=&membershipnumber=&societyetocsession=.

Simon Neubauer, Jean-Jacques Hublin and Philipp Gunz. 2018. "The evolution of modern human brain shape." *Science Advances* 4 (1).

Simone G. Shamay-Tsoory, Meytal Fischer, Jonathan Dvash, Hagai Harari, Nufar Perach-Bloom, Yechiel Levkovitz. 2009. "Intranasal Administration of Oxytocin Increases Envy and Schadenfreude (Gloating)." *Biological Psychiatry* 66 (9): 864-870. Accessed 7 30, 2018. https://sciencedirect.com/science/article/pii/s0006322309007628.

Simon-Thomas, Emiliana, Dacher Keltner, Disa Sauter, Lara Sinicropi-Yao, and Anna Abramson. 2009. "The voice conveys specific emotions: Evidence from vocal burst displays." *Emotion* 9 (6): 838-846. Accessed 6 26, 2018. http://psycnet.apa.org/journals/emo/9/6/838.pdf.

Sorrells, SF, MF Paredes, A Cebrian-Silla, K Sandoval, D Qi, KW Kelley, D James, et al. n.d. "Human hippocampal neurogenesis drops sharply in children to undetectable levels in adults." *Nature* 555 (7696): 377-381. Accessed 10 29, 2018.

Steve Ramirez1, Xu Liu1, Pei-Ann Lin1, Junghyup Suh1, Michele Pignatelli1, Roger L. Redondo, Tomás J. Ryan, Susumu Tonegawa. 2013. "Creating a False Memory in the Hippocampus." *Science* 387-391.

Suchak, Malini, Timothy M. Eppley, Matthew W. Campbell, and Frans B.M. de Waal. 2014. "Ape duos and trios: spontaneous cooperation with free partner choice in chimpanzees." *Animal Behaviour* 2: e417. Accessed 7 31, 2018.

Sull, Donald N., Rebecca Homkes, and Charles Sull. 2015. "Why strategy execution unravels– and what to do about it." *Harvard Business Review* 93 (3): 13. Accessed 12 14, 2018. https://dialnet.unirioja.es/servlet/articulo?codigo=5546365.

n.d. *System 1 VS System 2.* Accessed 6 29, 2018. http://upfrontanalytics.com/market-research-system-1-vs-system-2-decision-making/.

Tammi R.A. Kral, Brianna S.Schuylera, Jeanette A.Mumford, Melissa A.Rosenkranza, Antoine Lutz, Richard J.Davidson. 2018. "Impact of short- and long-term mindfulness meditation training on amygdala reactivity to emotional stimuli." *NeuroImage* 181: 301-313.

TEDTalks. 2015. "You can grow new brain cells. Here's how | Sandrine Thuret." October 30. https://youtu.be/B_tjKYvEzi1.

2018. *The Dress.* August 12. https://en.wikipedia.org/wiki/The_dress.

TheFreeDictionary.com. 2018. *EADGBE.* October 17. https://acronyms.thefreedictionary.com/EADGBE.

Thomas P. K. Breckel, Christiane M. Thiel, Edward T. Bullmore, Andrew Zalesky, Ameera X. Patel, Carsten Giessing. 2013. "Long-Term Effects of Attentional Performance on Functional Brain Network Topology." *PLOS One.*

Toepfer, Steven M., Kelly E. Cichy, and Patti Peters. 2012. "Letters of Gratitude: Further Evidence for Author Benefits." *Journal of Happiness Studies* 13 (1): 187-201. Accessed 8 2, 2018. https://link.springer.com/article/10.1007/s10902-011-9257-7.

Tom M.McLellana, John A.Caldwell, Harris R.Lieberman. 2016. "A review of caffeine's effects on cognitive, physical and occupational performance."

Elvevier 71: 294-312. doi:https://doi.org/10.1016/j.neubiorev.2016.09.001.

Treadway, Michael T., Joshua W. Buckholtz, Ronald L. Cowan, Neil D. Woodward, Rui Li, Mohammad Sib Ansari, Ronald M. Baldwin, Ashley N. Schwartzman, Robert M. Kessler, and David H. Zald. 2012. "Dopaminergic Mechanisms of Individual Differences in Human Effort-Based Decision-Making." *The Journal of Neuroscience* 32 (18): 6170-6176. Accessed 8 7, 2018. http://jneurosci.org/content/32/18/6170.

Trivers, Robert. 1971. "The Evolution of Reciprocal Altruism." *Quarlerly Review of Biology,* March: 35-57. https://www.researchgate.net/publication/230818222_The_Evolution_of_Reciprocal_Altruism.

Tsang, Jo-Ann. 2006. "BRIEF REPORT Gratitude and prosocial behaviour: An experimental test of gratitude." *Cognition & Emotion* 20 (1): 138-148. Accessed 11 14, 2018. https://tandfonline.com/doi/abs/10.1080/02699930500172341.

UC Davis Health. 2015. *Gratitude is good medicine* . November 25. https://www.ucdmc.ucdavis.edu/welcome/features/2015-2016/11/20151125_gratitude.html.

University of Oregon. 2017. *Journaling inspires altruism through an attitude of gratitude.* December 14. https://www.sciencedaily.com/releases/2017/12/171214100848.htm.

University of Pennsylvania School of Medicine. 2018. *One in four Americans develop insomnia each year: 75 percent of those with insomnia recover.* June 5. https://www.sciencedaily.com/releases/2018/06/180605154114.htm.

Uvnäs-Moberg, K., Handlin, L., & Petersson, M. 2014. "Self-soothing behaviors with particular reference to oxytocin release induced by non-noxious sensory stimulation." *Frontiers in Psychology 5* 1529.

V Gallese, C Keysers, G Rizzolatti. 2004. "A unifying view of the basis of social cognition." *Trends in cognitive sciences* 396-403.

Vieth, Erich. 2006. *Who first invented the golden rule?* August 18. http://dangerousintersection.org/2006/08/18/who-first-invented-the-golden-rule/comment-page-1/.

Vroom, V.H., Deci. 1983. *Management and Motivation.* Penguin 1983.

Watts, Barry D. 1996. *9. "Situation Awareness" in Air-to-Air Combat and Friction.* Accessed 9 6, 2018. https://questia.com/library/journal/1g1-126490761/9-situation-awareness-in-air-to-air-combat-and.

Watts, Tyler W., Greg J. Duncan, and Haonan Quan. 2018. "Revisiting the Marshmallow Test: A Conceptual Replication Investigating Links Between Early Delay of Gratification and Later Outcomes." *Psychological Science.* Accessed 10 11, 2018.

Wee, Tré, interview by Tré Wee. 2018. *Going First - The origin story (Feat. Gabrielle Reece)* (March 23). https://anchor.fm/betahuman/episodes/13--Going-First---The-origin-story-Feat--Gabrielle-Reece-e17ij4/a-a2q9r3.

Williams, Lisa A., and Monica Y. Bartlett. 2015. "Warm thanks: gratitude expression facilitates social affiliation in new relationships via perceived warmth." *Emotion* 15 (1): 1-5. Accessed 8 1, 2018. https://ncbi.nlm.nih.gov/pubmed/25111881.

Wood, Alex M., Stephen Joseph, Joanna Lloyd, and Samuel Atkins. 2009. "Gratitude influences sleep through the mechanism of pre-sleep cognitions." *Journal of Psychosomatic Research* 66 (1): 43-48. Accessed 8 1, 2018. https://sciencedirect.com/science/article/pii/s0022399908004224.

Xie, Lulu, Hongyi Kang, Qiwu Xu, Michael J. Chen, Yonghong Liao, Meenakshisundaram Thiyagarajan, John O'Donnell, et al. 2013. "Sleep Drives Metabolite Clearance from the Adult Brain." *Science* 342 (6156): 373-377. Accessed 8 22, 2018. http://www2.neuroscience.umn.edu/eanwebsite/pdf gjclub/science 342 373 2013.pdf.

Yaara Yeshurun, Stephen Swanson, Erez Simony, Janice Chen, Christina Lazaridi, Christopher J. Honey, and Uri Hasson. 2017. "Same Story, Different Story: The Neural Representation of Interpretive Frameworks." *Psychological Science* 307-319. https://europepmc.org/articles/pmc5348256.

Young, Dr. Larry, interview by Jesse Lawler. 2018. *Department of Psychiatry Emory University School of Medicine* (February 09).

Zagorski, Nick. 2016. *New Evidence for Classic 'Synaptic Pruning' Hypothesis of Schizophrenia.* March 17. doi:https://doi.org/10.1176/appi.pn.2016.3b51.

Zak, Paul J. 2017. "The Neuroscience of Trust." *Harvard Business Review,* January-February: 84-90.

Zak, Paul J. 2018. "The neuroscience of high-trust organizations." *Consulting Psychology Journal: Practice and Research* 70 (1): 45-58. Accessed 7 10, 2018. http://psycnet.apa.org/record/2018-09962-004.

—. 2017. *Trust Factor: The Science of Creating High-Performance Companies.* Accessed 11 12, 2018. https://amazon.com/trust-factor-creating-high-performance-companies/dp/0814437664.

Zilioli, Samuele, Davide Ponzi, Andrea Henry, and Dario Maestripieri. 2015. *Testosterone, Cortisol and Empathy: Evidence for the Dual-Hormone Hypothesis.* Accessed 11 12, 2018. https://link.springer.com/article/10.1007/s40750-014-0017-x.

www.ingramcontent.com/pod-product-compliance
Lightning Source LLC
Chambersburg PA
CBHW062025210326
41519CB00060B/7075